MEGAN S. SCHULER, MICHAEL S. DUNBAR,
ELIZABETH ROTH, JOSHUA BRESLAU

The State of Health and Health Care for LGBTQ+ Veterans

Differences Among Sexual and Gender Minority Veterans, by Identity and State Policy Climate, 2015–2021

For more information on this publication, visit **www.rand.org/t/RRA1363-9**.

About RAND

RAND is a research organization that develops solutions to public policy challenges to help make communities throughout the world safer and more secure, healthier and more prosperous. RAND is nonprofit, nonpartisan, and committed to the public interest. To learn more about RAND, visit www.rand.org.

Research Integrity

Our mission to help improve policy and decisionmaking through research and analysis is enabled through our core values of quality and objectivity and our unwavering commitment to the highest level of integrity and ethical behavior. To help ensure our research and analysis are rigorous, objective, and nonpartisan, we subject our research publications to a robust and exacting quality-assurance process; avoid both the appearance and reality of financial and other conflicts of interest through staff training, project screening, and a policy of mandatory disclosure; and pursue transparency in our research engagements through our commitment to the open publication of our research findings and recommendations, disclosure of the source of funding of published research, and policies to ensure intellectual independence. For more information, visit www.rand.org/about/research-integrity.

RAND's publications do not necessarily reflect the opinions of its research clients and sponsors.

Library of Congress Cataloging-in-Publication Data is available for this publication.
ISBN: 978-1-9774-1332-1

Cover Photo: U.S. Department of Veterans Affairs

About This Report

The U.S. government has re-affirmed its commitment to improving health and well-being for lesbian, gay, bisexual, transgender, queer, and other sexual and gender minority (LGBTQ+) veterans. As with LGBTQ+ civilians, LGBTQ+ veterans can have distinct needs and challenges when accessing timely and appropriate healthcare. Previous studies have documented disparities in health care access and health-related outcomes for LGBTQ+ veterans relative to their cisgender and heterosexual peers. However, many studies of LGBTQ+ veterans' health disparities focus on limited constructs or domains (e.g., mental health), and much of the existing literature does not consider within-group differences (e.g., by sexual or gender identity). Thus, we lack a comprehensive understanding of how and for whom different disparities may manifest for sexual and gender minority veterans, which has implications for directing resources to those individuals who may benefit most from targeted efforts to improve health and well-being. Furthermore, recent work has documented associations between state LGBTQ+ policy climates (e.g., presence of employment nondiscrimination policies, legislation related to provision of and access to gender-affirming health care) and mental health, substance use, and health behaviors among LGBTQ+ individuals. Such policies might hinder federal efforts to remove treatment barriers for and better support LGBTQ+ veterans. However, few studies examine the impact of recent state policies on health-related outcomes for LGBTQ+ veterans.

To address these gaps, in this report, we use large, representative datasets (2015–2021 Behavioral Risk Factor Surveillance System data) to describe prevalence estimates of health-related outcomes across multiple domains (health care access and affordability, general health, substance use, and chronic conditions) for sexual and gender minority veterans relative to their heterosexual and cisgender veteran peers. We also examine associations between state LGBTQ+ policy climates and health-related outcomes among LGBTQ+ veterans. We discuss implications for ongoing efforts to improve health and well-being for LGBTQ+ veterans, including sustained actions to ensure that all LGBTQ+ veterans are able to access necessary care and use the full scope of benefits for which they are eligible.

About RAND

RAND is a research organization that develops solutions to public policy challenges to help make communities throughout the world safer and more secure, healthier and more prosperous. RAND is nonprofit, nonpartisan, and committed to the public interest. To learn more about RAND, visit www.rand.org

The RAND Epstein Family Veterans Policy Research Institute

The RAND Epstein Family Veterans Policy Research Institute is dedicated to conducting innovative, evidence-based research and analysis to improve the lives of those who have served in the U.S. military. Building on decades of interdisciplinary expertise at RAND, the institute prioritizes creative, equitable, and inclusive solutions and interventions that meet the needs of diverse veteran populations while engaging and empowering those who support them. For more information about the RAND Epstein Family Veterans Policy Research Institute, visit veterans.rand.org. Questions about this report or about the RAND Epstein Family Veterans Policy Research Institute should be directed to veteranspolicy@rand.org.

RAND Health Care

RAND Health Care, a division of RAND, promotes healthier societies by improving health care systems in the United States and other countries. We do this by providing health care decisionmakers, practitioners, and consumers with actionable, rigorous, objective evidence to support their most complex decisions. For more information, see www.rand.org/health-care.

Funding

Funding for this publication was made possible by a generous gift from Daniel J. Epstein through the Epstein Family Foundation, which established the RAND Epstein Family Veterans Policy Research Institute in 2021.

Acknowledgments

We would like to thank Carrie Farmer and Rajeev Ramchand for their guidance and input on study design. Additionally, we thank our peer reviewers, John Blosnich and Daniel Siconolfi, for their invaluable feedback on this report.

Summary

Lesbian, gay, bisexual, transgender, queer, and other sexual and gender minority (LGBTQ+) veterans, as with LGBTQ+ civilians, may experience distinct health care needs and challenges when accessing timely and appropriate health care. Previous studies have documented disparities in health care access and health-related outcomes for LGBTQ+ veterans relative to their cisgender and heterosexual peers, but few studies have systematically reported on differences both by sexual identity and gender identity for multiple health-related outcomes. Thus, we lack data on whether and how disparities may manifest for specific groups of LGBTQ+ veterans; these data have implications for informing efforts to optimally assist groups who may have distinct needs. Furthermore, in the context of dynamic social and political climates surrounding LGBTQ+ rights and health care in many states and localities, little is known about how policies affecting LGBTQ+ individuals may contribute to health-related outcomes for LGBTQ+ veterans. Such data can provide insight into the extent to which such policies might affect ongoing federal efforts to improve health and well-being for sexual and gender minority veterans.

In this report, we use large, representative datasets (2015–2021 Behavioral Risk Factor Surveillance System [BRFSS] data) to describe prevalence estimates of health-related outcomes across multiple domains (health care access and affordability, general health status, substance use, and chronic conditions or diagnoses) for LGBTQ+ U.S. veterans. We also examine associations between state LGBTQ+ policy climates and health-related outcomes among LGBTQ+ veterans.

In age-adjusted prevalence estimates from the 2015–2021 BRFSS data, female and male sexual minority veterans—i.e., veterans who identify as lesbian, gay, bisexual, or another nonheterosexual identity—showed poorer health-related outcomes in a variety of domains when compared with age-adjusted heterosexual peers of the same sex. Similarly, transgender veterans—i.e., veterans whose gender identity or expression differs from their assigned sex at birth—showed poorer outcomes in multiple domains relative to their cisgender peers. For example:

- Among both female and male veterans, those who identify as bisexual or another nonheterosexual identity were significantly more likely to report having been unable to afford medical care in the past year than heterosexual veterans of the same sex. Transgender veterans were nearly twice as likely to report unaffordability of medical care compared with cisgender veterans.
- Lesbian or gay female veterans and gay male veterans were significantly more likely to report current cigarette smoking than heterosexual female and male veterans, respectively. Transgender veterans were significantly more likely than cisgender veterans to report current smoking.

- Male and female sexual minority veterans had significantly elevated odds of reporting a lifetime history of major depressive disorder when compared with their heterosexual peers. Similarly, transgender veterans were significantly more likely to report a lifetime history of depression when compared with cisgender veterans.
- Among both female and male veterans, all sexual minority groups were more likely to rate their mental health as "not good" for more than two weeks in the past month than their heterosexual peers were. Transgender veterans were nearly twice as likely to report that their mental health was not good for more than two weeks in the past month than cisgender veterans.
- Among male veterans, all sexual minority groups were more likely to have had a stroke than heterosexual male veterans. The lifetime prevalence of stroke was three times higher among transgender veterans when compared with cisgender veterans.
- Among both female and male veterans, all sexual minority groups were more likely than heterosexual veterans to have a lifetime diagnosis of chronic obstructive pulmonary disease (COPD), emphysema, or chronic bronchitis. Lifetime prevalence of COPD, emphysema, or chronic bronchitis was more than twice as high among transgender veterans than cisgender veterans.
- Lesbian or gay female veterans, gay male veterans, and bisexual male veterans were significantly more likely to have a lifetime diabetes diagnosis than their heterosexual veteran peers were. Transgender veterans were more likely to report a lifetime diabetes diagnosis than cisgender veterans.

Among LGBTQ+ veterans, living in a state with a more favorable LGBTQ+ policy climate (compared with a negative LGBTQ+ policy climate)—as rated by the Movement Advancement Project's 2015 state policy ratings—was associated with better health-related outcomes (in 2015–2017 BRFSS data) in some domains. For example,

- State LGBTQ+ policy climate was associated with some indicators of health care access. LGBTQ+ policy climate in 2015 was associated with health insurance status, such that individuals residing in states with more favorable policy ratings (rated as low, medium, or high favorability) were significantly more likely to report having health insurance compared with LGBTQ+ veterans residing in states with a negative LGBTQ+ policy rating. Additionally, individuals in states with more favorable LGBTQ+ policy climates were more likely than those in states with a negative policy rating to report having had a check-up visit with a health care provider in the past year.
- Few statistically significant associations between state LGBTQ+ policy climate and outcomes were observed in other domains. Individuals residing in states with low, medium, or high policy ratings were less likely to report current cigarette smoking compared with those in states with a negative LGBTQ+ policy climate in 2015. In contrast, individuals residing in states with medium policy climates were more likely than those in

states with negative policy climates to report a lifetime history of angina or coronary heart disease.

In this report, we add to the growing body of literature indicating that there are significant disparities in access to health care and health-related outcomes across multiple domains for LGBTQ+ veterans compared with their heterosexual and cisgender counterparts. Our findings underscore the importance and urgency of efforts to improve health services and outcomes for LGBTQ+ veterans, including sustained actions to ensure that all LGBTQ+ veterans can access needed health care services and use the full scope of benefits for which they are eligible.

Contents

Figures and Tables

Figures

Tables

CHAPTER 1

Introduction

Lesbian, gay, bisexual, transgender and other sexual and gender minority (LGBTQ+)[1] members of the U.S. military have faced a long history of discrimination and exclusion from the benefits of their service while on active duty and as veterans (Burgess, Klemt Craig, and Klemmer, 2021; National Defense Research Institute, 2010). As of this writing in early 2024, LGBTQ+ rights remain contested inside and outside the military (Robertson, 2024; Thomas, 2023; Williams, 2023), complicating such basic activities as obtaining health care for an estimated 1 million LGBTQ+ veterans (U.S. Department of Veterans Affairs, 2022). Despite recognition by the military that prior exclusionary policies—such as *Don't Ask Don't Tell* (DADT) and prohibitions on serving for individuals with "transgender conditions" (Schaefer et al., 2016)—were unjustly discriminatory, LGBTQ+ veterans who were discharged from service when those policies were in effect continue to be excluded from veterans' benefits (Dwyer and Herndon, 2023; Kheel, 2023; Wiessner, 2023). More broadly, nationally and in state legislatures, there have been efforts to renew restrictions on health care for transgender individuals (Human Rights Campaign, 2023; Shane, 2023), and some states have passed legislation that could limit public visibility of and legal protections for LGBTQ+ individuals (Davis, 2023; Human Rights Campaign, 2023; Lenson, 2015). These negative trends in social climate for LGBTQ+ individuals in some states raise concerns about the impact that historical and current discrimination and exclusion have on LGBTQ+ veterans. Recognizing these trends and their potential harms, the Biden-Harris administration has affirmed a commitment to removing barriers to health services for LGBTQ+ veterans (White House, 2022).

To inform policy and future research, we examine disparities in access to and use of health care, mental and physical health, behavioral health (substance use), and chronic health con-

---

[1] The National Institutes of Health defines *sexual and gender minority populations* as individuals

> who identify as lesbian, gay, bisexual, asexual, transgender, Two-Spirit, queer, and/or intersex. Individuals with same-sex or -gender attractions or behaviors and those with variations in sex characteristics are also included. These populations also encompass those who do not self-identify with one of these terms but whose sexual orientation, gender identity or expression, or reproductive development is characterized by non-binary constructs of sexual orientation, gender, and/or sex (National Institutes of Health, 2024).

Sexual orientation refers to one's sexual attraction, sexual behavior, and sexual identity (e.g., identifying as lesbian, gay, bisexual). *Gender identity* refers to one's identity with or sense of gender (e.g., being a man, woman, nonbinary). *Transgender* refers to an individual who identifies with a gender that differs from the sex assigned to them at birth.

ditions between LGBTQ+ veterans and their heterosexual and cisgender peers using a large population-based sample. Disparities in these domains have been identified in prior studies of LGBTQ+ veterans (Blosnich et al., 2013; Carey et al., 2022; Kondo et al., 2017; Mark et al., 2019), although the magnitude and scope of differences may vary depending on specific group comparisons. For example, one study by Downing and colleagues examined differences in health-related outcomes for transgender and cisgender veterans using nationally representative data from the 2014–2016 Behavioral Risk Factor Surveillance System (BRFSS) and found relatively few health-related disparities for transgender veterans compared with their cisgender peers (Downing et al., 2018). However, the existing literature on LGBTQ+ veterans' health is relatively limited, and previous work has been limited by such factors as small sample sizes and lack of data on sexual and gender identity and related constructs. There is an urgent need for additional research to improve understanding of how health-related disparities may manifest for diverse LGBTQ+ veterans (Draper, 2020). In this report, we address several limitations of prior research. First, we examine a variety of outcomes within the context of a single study, enabling comparisons that can help identify major issues of concern. Second, recognizing the growing body of evidence that clearly indicates that LGBTQ+ individuals are not a monolith (Brown and Jones, 2014; Committee on Lesbian, Gay, Bisexual and Transgender Health Issues and Research Gaps and Opportunities, 2011; Patterson, Sepúlveda, and White, 2020), we examine heterogeneity across LGBTQ+ subgroups and intersections of LGBTQ+ identity and gender. Because treatment use, needs, and barriers may vary considerably across LGBTQ+ individuals (e.g., for men versus women or for transgender versus cisgender individuals) (Brown and Jones, 2014; Kondo et al., 2017; Patterson, Sepúlveda, and White, 2020), this is an important knowledge gap. Third, most evidence on veteran health comes from Veterans Health Administration (VHA) samples, yet most veterans receive care outside the VHA system (Meffert et al., 2019). Studies using large, national epidemiological samples that include diverse veterans are needed to understand heterogeneity in health and service use among LGBTQ+ veterans and differences in relation to their non-LGBTQ+ peers.

Given the resurgence of legislation related to LGBTQ+ health and identity in recent years, the relationship between the policy environment as an indicator of social inclusivity and disparities related to LGBTQ+ identity is of increasing importance (Blosnich et al., 2016; Committee on Lesbian, Gay, Bisexual and Transgender Health Issues and Research Gaps and Opportunities, 2011; Hatzenbuehler, Keyes, and Hasin, 2009; Meyer, 2003; National Institutes of Health, Sexual and Gender Minority Research Office, 2021; Patterson, Sepúlveda, and White, 2020). A 2023 study by White and colleagues that used data from the BRFSS found that state-level LGBTQ+-inclusivity (using the 2018 Human Rights Campaign State Equality Index) correlated with LGBTQ+ individuals' well-being and health behaviors, such that LGBTQ+ individuals residing in states with lower inclusivity ratings were significantly more likely to report having poorer overall health, having a greater number of days with poor mental health, and had higher odds of cigarette smoking and heavy drinking (White et al., 2022). However, comparatively little is known about how state-level LGBTQ+ policy climate may affect health and service use for LGBTQ+ veterans. For example, one study by Blosnich and colleagues used administrative data, the 2013 Human Rights Campaign Municipality Equality Index ratings, and information on state employment nondiscrimination protections to examine associations between policy climate and mental and behavioral health outcomes in a sample of transgender veterans who received care through the VHA. The authors found that patients residing in states with nondiscrimination protections that included transgender status or gender identity had lower odds of mood disorder diagnoses compared to those living in states without such protections (Blosnich et al., 2016). Examining the effect of state LGBTQ+ policy climate on veterans' health disparities has critical and timely implications for efforts to support health and well-being for LGBTQ+ veterans. Contemporary research is needed to understand the impact of policy environments on LGBTQ+ veterans' health, particularly in the context of proposed and enacted legislative actions that may reduce protections for LGBTQ+ individuals (American Civil Liberties Union, 2024; Human Rights Campaign, 2023).

In this report, we use pooled data from large representative datasets (from the 2015–2021 BRFSS) to characterize differences in healthcare access and health status for LGBTQ+ veterans across multiple domains (i.e., health care access, general health status, substance use, and health conditions and diagnoses). Additionally, among LGBTQ+ veterans, we examine associations between state-level LGBTQ+ policy climate in 2015 and health-related outcomes in pooled 2015–2021 BRFSS data.

Data Sources and Measures

The study used data from the 2015–2021 BRFSS and 2015 Movement Advancement Project (MAP) state LGBTQ+ policy ratings.

BRFSS Data

BRFSS is a state-based surveillance system in the United States that collects data on health-related risk behaviors, chronic health conditions, and use of preventive services among U.S. adult residents. BRFSS is conducted annually by the Centers for Disease Control and Prevention (CDC) in all 50 states, Washington, D.C., and three U.S. territories (Guam, Puerto Rico, and the Virgin Islands) in collaboration with state health departments. BRFSS response rates are shown in Appendix C. BRFSS is one of the largest ongoing health surveys in the world; its data are collected from more than 400,000 adults each year using telephone interviews.

The BRFSS survey consists of three components: (1) the core BRFSS survey items (states must use without modification); (2) optional BRFSS modules on specific topics of interest (states must use without modification); and (3) any additional state-added questions (optional). The core BRFSS survey collects information on a wide range of topics, including tobacco use, physical activity, nutrition, alcohol consumption, chronic health conditions, and use of preventive services (CDC, 2023). Optional BRFSS modules are designed to collect information on specific topics of interest (e.g., sexual orientation and gender identity, adverse childhood experiences, family planning, cancer survivorship, cognitive decline, tobacco cessation).

Health-related outcomes: The present study focuses on multiple health-related outcomes assessed in the core BRFSS survey from 2015 through 2021. We selected these outcomes based on availability (e.g., inclusion and relative consistency in item language and interpretation across all annual datasets), data quality and interpretability, relevance to characterizing health care access and health status, and alignment with outcomes reported in the existing literature (Carey et al., 2022; Substance Abuse and Mental Health Services Administration, 2023). Table 1.1 shows the health-related outcomes and corresponding source items in 2015–2021 BRFSS data examined in this study. Wording for some items changed across BRFSS years although changes were minor and items yield comparable outcomes across years. Outcomes were dichotomized to generate prevalence estimates and facilitate interpretation.

Veteran status: Respondents were classified as veterans on the basis of an affirmative response to the core BRFSS item that asks: "Have you ever served on active duty in the United States Armed Forces, either in the regular military or in a National Guard or military reserve unit?" We note that this population might include some individuals who are currently on active duty or reserve, because the BRFSS sampling frame includes active-duty military service members living in private residences (i.e., not on a military base).[2] BRFSS assessed current military status until 2010. In pooled data from 2015–2021, we identified 185,944 veterans.

Sex: Sex was classified as male or female on the basis of the recorded sex variable in BRFSS. Assessment of sex in BRFSS changed across our study years (see Appendix D for details). In 2016–2021, respondents were asked to self-report their sex as male or female. In 2015, interviewers were instructed to record respondent sex (as male or female, presumably based on vocal timbre) and instructed to "Ask [respondent sex] only if necessary." We note that this variable likely contains some measurement error. First, the BRFSS sex variable purports to measure the construct of biological sex ("sex at birth"), but the ambiguous wording of the question (i.e., "Are you male or female") might lead some respondents to answer with respect to their current gender identity rather than their biological sex. Additionally, as prior studies have shown, interviewer-recorded sex classification based on vocal timbre has been shown to result in misclassification with respect to biological sex, particularly for transgender individuals (Cicero et al., 2020; Riley et al., 2017).

---

2   According to the American Community Survey, there were 17,924,662 veterans in 2018. According to the Defense Manpower Data Center, in 2018, there were 1,345,550 active-duty military members (including active-duty Coast Guard) and an additional 802,842 reserve and guard members. Approximately two-thirds of active-duty families live off base, as do the nearly all reserve and guard members. We estimate that approximately $2/3 \cdot (1,345,550) + 802,842 = 1,699,875$ active-duty service members and reserve and guard members were living off base and may have been eligible for participation in the BRFSS survey. The proportion of all community-dwelling individuals who have ever served that are still active/reserve can be approximated as $1,699,875 / (1,699,875 + 17,924,662) = 8.6$ percent. Thus, we estimate that approximately 8.6 percent of respondents stating yes to the BRFSS "ever served" item may be active duty or reserve rather than veterans.

TABLE 1.1

Health-Related Outcome Variables Derived from 2015-2021 BRFSS Data

Domain and Construct	Outcome Variable Definition	BRFSS source item(s) *Item Text (Variable Name) [Year]*
Health care access and affordability		
Checkup (routine care visit) in past year	Had routine checkup within past year (yes)	• About how long has it been since you last visited a doctor for a routine checkup? (CHECKUP1) [2015–2021]
Has a personal care provider	Endorsed having a personal healthcare provider (yes)	• Do you have one person you think of as your personal doctor or health care provider? (PERSDOC2) [2015–2020] • Do you have one person (or a group of doctors) that you think of as your personal health care provider? (PERSDOC3) [2021]
Health insurance status	Has health insurance (i.e., employer, private, public, VA [Veterans Affairs], or other source) (yes)	• Do you have any kind of health care coverage, including health insurance, prepaid plans such as HMOs, or government plans such as Medicare, or Indian Health Service? (HLTHPLN1) [2015–2020] • What is the current primary source of your health insurance? (PRIMINSR) [2021]
Health care affordability	Could not afford medical care in the past 12 months	• Was there a time in the past 12 months when you needed to see a doctor but could not because of cost? (MEDCOST) [2015–2020] • Was there a time in the past 12 months when you needed to see a doctor but could not because you could not afford it? (MEDCOST1) [2021]
General health status		
Subjective overall health	Self-reported health rated excellent or very good	• Would you say that in general your health is: Excellent; Very Good; Good; Fair; Poor? (GENHLTH) [2015–2021]
Functional impairments	Health interfered with daily activities for 14+ days in the past month	• During the past 30 days, for about how many days did poor physical or mental health keep you from doing your usual activities, such as self-care, work, or recreation? (POORHLTH) [2015–2021]
Poor subjective mental health	Mental health not good for 14+ days in the past month	• Now thinking about your mental health, which includes stress, depression, and problems with emotions, for how many days during the past 30 days was your mental health not good? (MNTHLTH) [2015–2021]
Poor subjective physical health	Physical health not good for 14+ days in the past month	• Now thinking about your physical health, which includes physical illness and injury, for how many days during the past 30 days was your physical health not good? (PHYSHLTH) [2015–2021]

Table 1.1—Continued

Domain and Construct	Outcome Variable Definition	BRFSS source item(s) Item Text (Variable Name) [Year]
Exercise	Any exercise in past 30 days	• During the past month, other than your regular job, did you participate in any physical activities or exercises such as running, calisthenics, golf, gardening, or walking for exercise? (EXERANY2) [2015–2021]
18.5 ≤ BMI <25 (body mass index [BMI] in normal range)[a]	Weight in normal range (18.5 ≤ BMI < 25)	• BRFSS calculated variable: BMI category, based on respondent Height and Weight (_BMI5CAT) [2015–2021]
Substance use		
Cigarette smoking	Current smoking (yes)	• Do you now smoke cigarettes every day, some days, or not at all? (SMOKDAY2) [2015–2021]
Alcohol use	Any current alcohol use (One or more drinks in the past month)	• During the past 30 days, how many days per week or per month did you have at least one drink of any alcoholic beverage such as beer, wine, a malt beverage or liquor? (ALCDAY5) [2015–2021]
Binge drinking[b]	Binge drinking one 1 or more days in the past 30 days	• Considering all types of alcoholic beverages, how many times during the past 30 days did you have 5 or more drinks for men or 4 or more drinks for women on an occasion? (DRNK3GE5) [2015–2021]
Heavy alcohol use[b]	Current (past 30-day) heavy alcohol use	• BRFSS calculated variable: Heavy drinking status defined as having more than 14 drinks per week (men) and more than 7 drinks per week (women) (_RFDRHV5) [2015–2017] • BRFSS calculated variable: Heavy drinking status defined as having more than 14 drinks per week (men) and more than 7 drinks per week (women) (_RFDRHV6) [2018] • BRFSS calculated variable: Heavy drinking status defined as having more than 14 drinks per week (men) and more than 7 drinks per week (women) (_RFDRHV7) [2019–2021]
Chronic health conditions		
History of stroke	Ever told had stroke (yes)	• (Ever told) (you had) a stroke? (CVDSTRK3) [2015–2021]
History of coronary heart disease (CHD)	Ever told had angina or CHD (yes)	• (Ever told) (you had) angina or CHD? (CVDCRHD4) [2015–2021]
History of heart attack	Ever told had a heart attack (yes)	• (Ever told) you had a heart attack, also called a myocardial infarction? (CVDINFR4) [2015–2021]

Table 1.1—Continued

Domain and Construct	Outcome Variable Definition	BRFSS source item(s) *Item Text (Variable Name) [Year]*
History of depression	Ever told had depressive disorder (yes)	• (Ever told) you that you have a depressive disorder, including depression, major depression, dysthymia, or minor depression? (ADDEPEV2) [2015–2018] • (Ever told) (you had) a depressive disorder (including depression, major depression, dysthymia, or minor depression)? (ADDEPEV3) [2019–2021]
History of chronic respiratory disease	Ever told had COPD, emphysema, or chronic bronchitis (yes)	• (Ever told) you have chronic obstructive pulmonary disease (COPD), emphysema, or chronic bronchitis? (CHCCOPD1) [2015–2018] • (Ever told) (you had) COPD, emphysema, or chronic bronchitis? (CHCCOPD2) [2019–2020] • (Ever told) (you had) COPD, emphysema, or chronic bronchitis? (CHCCOPD3) [2021]
History of asthma	Ever told had asthma (yes)	• (Ever told) (you had) asthma? (ASTHMA3) [2015–2021]
History of skin cancer	Ever told had skin cancer (yes)	• (Ever told) (you had) skin cancer? (CHCSCNCR) [2015–2021]
History of diabetes	Ever told had diabetes (yes)	• (Ever told) you have diabetes? (DIABETE3) [2015–2018] • (Ever told) (you had) diabetes? (DIABETE4) [2019–2021]
History of kidney disease	Ever told had kidney disease (yes)	• (Ever told) you have kidney disease? (CHCKIDNY) [2015–2017] • (Ever told) you have kidney disease? (CHCKIDNY1) [2018] • Not including kidney stones, bladder infection, or incontinence, were you ever told you had kidney disease? (CHCKIDNY2) [2019–2021]
History of arthritis or autoimmune conditions	Ever told had arthritis, rheumatoid arthritis, gout, lupus or fibromyalgia (yes)	• (Ever told) you have some form of arthritis, rheumatoid arthritis, gout, lupus, or fibromyalgia? (HAVARTH3) [2015–2018] • (Ever told) (you had) some form of arthritis, rheumatoid arthritis, gout, lupus, or fibromyalgia? (HAVARTH4) [2019–2021]

SOURCE: Uses information from CDC, 2023.
NOTE: HMO = health maintenance organization;

[a] Definition of normal range BMI uses information from Purnell, 2023.

[b] Sex-based thresholds for binge drinking and heavy alcohol use are based on the BRFSS sex variable (male or female). Per BRFSS documentation, if sex at birth is reported (via optional BRFSS module) and differs from sex, then sex at birth is used when calculating these derived variables.

Sexual identity: Data on sexual identity come from the optional BRFSS Sexual Orientation and Gender Identity (SOGI) module that was introduced in 2014 and was updated in 2018 (see Appendix D for details). This module may be added to the standard BRFSS questionnaire on a voluntary basis by state health departments.

In 2015–2017, sexual identity was assessed on the SOGI module with the item: "Do you consider yourself to be" with the response options "straight," "lesbian or gay," "bisexual," "other," or "don't know/not sure." In 2018–2021, sexual identity was assessed with the item: "Which of the following best represents how you think of yourself?" with response options "gay [male respondents]/lesbian or gay [female respondents]," "straight, that is, not gay," "bisexual," "something else," or "I don't know the answer." In our analyses, we examined four sexual identity groups based on these items: gay/lesbian, bisexual, other identity, and heterosexual. Individuals who responded "don't know/not sure" (2015–2017) or "I don't know the answer" (2018–2021), or who skipped this question were excluded from analyses examining sexual identity.

In 2015, 23 states and U.S. territories included the optional SOGI module; by 2021, the number had increased to 33. In pooled data from 2015–2021, our sample comprised 2,460 bisexual veterans, 2,350 lesbian or gay veterans, 1,566 veterans who identified as another sexual identity, and 179,568 heterosexual veterans. We note that both prior and subsequent to the introduction of the BRFSS optional SOGI module, some states collected SOGI data using their own state-specific SOGI module. In our analyses, we use sexual identity data only from the standard BRFSS optimal SOGI module and do not include data from state-specific SOGI questions.

Gender identity and transgender status: Transgender veterans were identified based on either (1) the transgender identity question in the optional BRFSS SOGI module (2015–2021) or (2) the optional BRFSS Sex at Birth module (2019–2021; see Appendix D for details). In the SOGI module, respondents are asked "Do you consider yourself to be transgender?" In our analyses, all individuals who responded "yes" were classified as transgender. We note that in the SOGI module, if respondents answer affirmatively, they are then able to identify as "transgender male-to-female," "transgender, female-to-male," or "transgender, gender nonconforming." We note that we were not able to examine differences among transgender respondents based on specific gender identities because of limited sample size.

In 2019, the optional Sex at Birth module was introduced; similar to the SOGI module, states may opt to add this module to the standard BRFSS questionnaire on a voluntary basis. This module asks "What was your sex at birth? Was it male or female?" In our analyses, we also classified individuals as transgender if their reported sex at birth did not match the BRFSS sex variable (e.g., sex recorded as male, sex at birth reported as female). All individuals who were not identified as transgender were classified as cisgender.

In 2015, 23 states and U.S. territories included the optional SOGI module; by 2021, the number had increased to 33. The Sex at Birth module was included by seven states in 2019 and ten in 2021. We identified 987 transgender veterans in pooled 2015–2021 BRFSS data.

Demographic covariates: In this report, we also used data on participant age (categories: ages 18 to 24, 25 to 34, 35 to 44, 45 to 54, 55 to 64, and 65 years or older), race and ethnicity (White only, Non-Hispanic; Black only, non-Hispanic; other race only, non-Hispanic; multiracial, non-Hispanic; Hispanic), and education (college degree or higher versus less than a college degree) as covariates in logistic regression models examining associations between state policy climate and health outcomes among LGBTQ+ veterans.

Movement Advancement Project State Policy Data

MAP's 2015 LGBTQ+ policy tallies (ratings) summarize a variety of LGBTQ+ state policies (e.g., relationship and parental recognition, nondiscrimination, healthcare, religious exemptions) to characterize overall state-level LGBTQ+ policy environment—i.e., the extent to which policy setting is protective or affirming for LGBTQ+ individuals—in the following categories: *negative* (n = 15 states), *low* (n = 13 states), *medium* (n = 10 states), or *high* (n = 12 states). Detailed methodology for MAP's policy ratings can be found in the 2015 report *Mapping LGBT Equality in America* (MAP, 2015). We note that MAP has also published data on state policy tallies in 2010 and 2020 (MAP, 2020), although state policy tallies in these years used different methodologies than in 2015; thus, state policy tally data in these years are not directly comparable with 2015 data. Because 2015 data coincide with the first year of available BRFSS data, we used publicly available MAP policy rating data from 2015 as an index of recent state LGBTQ+ climate. As described in the following sections, acknowledging that state policies change over time and that 2015 data may not accurately characterize recent state policy climate in later years of available BRFSS data, we report analyses with only 2015–2017 BRFSS data.

CHAPTER 2

Analyses

Prevalence Estimates and Statistical Tests of Differences, by Sexual and Gender Identity

In this report, we focus on examining two types of comparisons among U.S. veteran respondents in BRFSS data from 2015–2021. First, we examine differences by sexual identity, comparing heterosexual veterans with sexual minority veterans (i.e., veterans who identify as gay or lesbian, bisexual, or another sexual identity). We present sexual identity analyses stratified by sex (i.e., male or female) using prior research that indicates sex differences in a variety of health-related outcomes. Second, we examine differences by gender identity (i.e., between transgender veterans and cisgender veterans).

Because of differences in the age distributions of veterans by sex, sexual identity, and gender identity, we report age-adjusted prevalence estimates as our primary findings in the report (including all figures). When examining differences by sexual identity, we stratify by sex and standardize female sexual minority groups to female heterosexual veterans, allowing direct comparison across sexual identity groups within women. Similarly, we standardize male sexual minority groups to male heterosexual veterans. Age-adjusted prevalence estimates are not directly comparable across males and females because they are standardized to different populations (i.e., the female heterosexual veteran population is significantly younger than the male heterosexual veteran population). When examining differences by gender identity, we standardize the transgender group with the cisgender group for direct comparison.

All estimates presented in this report were calculated accounting for the BRFSS survey design and additionally included response weights for the optional SOGI and Sex at Birth modules. Comparisons of age-adjusted estimates across sexual identity and gender groups were performed using logistic regression. Differences in age-adjusted estimates were considered statistically significant at the $p < 0.05$ level.

Associations Between State LGBTQ+ Policy Climate and Health-Related Outcomes

Using BRFSS data and merged 2015 MAP state policy data, we conducted multiple logistic regression analyses to examine associations between 2015 state policy climate and health-related outcomes for LGBTQ+ veterans. In the subset of LGBTQ+ survey respondents, separate models examined associations between state policy climate (negative [reference group], low, medium, high) and each dichotomous outcome of interest. As noted previously, we used 2015 policy data from MAP because it is publicly available and coincides with the first year of BRFSS data (2015), which provides an index of recent state policy climate. However, because BRFSS data span 2015 to 2021, and because state policies may change over time (MAP, 2020), 2015 data may provide a poorer index of "recent" policy climate for later BRFSS survey years (e.g., 2018–2021) compared with earlier years (e.g., 2015–2017). Thus, to improve temporal alignment between MAP 2015 policy data and BRFSS data on health-related outcomes, we restricted analyses to BRFSS survey years 2015–2017. All models adjusted for survey year and respondent demographic characteristics (age, sex, race and ethnicity, and education).

Prevalence Estimates: Differences in Health-Related Outcomes, by Sexual and Gender Identity

In the following section, we show age-adjusted estimated prevalence estimates for health-related outcomes by sexual identity (heterosexual, gay or lesbian, bisexual, or another identity) in the BRFSS data for men and women veterans and by veterans' transgender status (transgender; cisgender). Full prevalence estimates and corresponding tests of significant group differences for all outcomes are shown in Tables A.1 through A.11 in Appendix A. In this section, we present prevalence estimates by outcome domain (health care access and affordability, general health status, substance use, and chronic health conditions). For each domain, we describe differences in veteran's prevalence estimates for each outcome of interest by sexual identity for men and women and subsequently by gender identity (transgender and cisgender veterans).

Health Care Access and Affordability

Figure 2.1 shows age-adjusted prevalence estimates for health care access and affordability outcomes for female and male veterans by sexual identity. The following significant group differences emerged:

- Bisexual female and male veterans were less likely to report having health insurance than heterosexual veteran peers. The prevalence of uninsurance among bisexual female veterans was nearly 10 percentage points lower than among heterosexual female veterans.
- Bisexual female veterans were less likely to have had a checkup in the past year compared with heterosexual female veterans.
- Bisexual female veterans and female veterans with other sexual identities were twice as likely to be unable to afford medical care in the past year when compared with heterosexual female veterans. Among male veterans, all sexual minority groups were more likely to be unable to afford medical care in the past year compared with heterosexual male veterans. Male veterans with other sexual identities were twice as likely to report unaffordability of care.

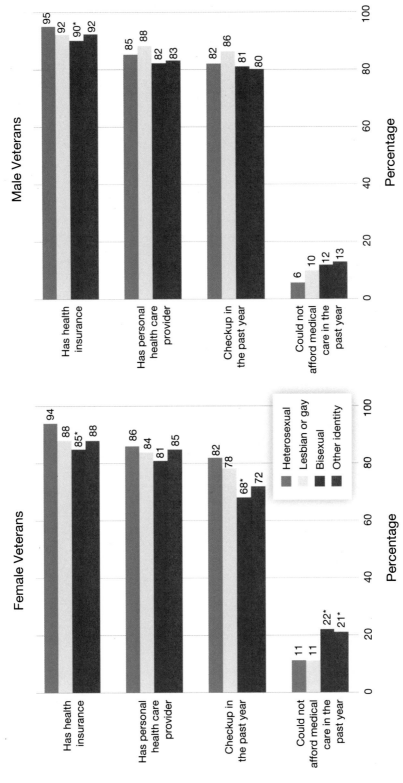

FIGURE 2.1
Health Care Access and Affordability Among Female and Male Veterans, by Sexual Identity

SOURCE: Uses BRFSS data from 2015–2021.
NOTE: Prevalence estimates among female sexual minority groups are age-standardized to the female heterosexual group for comparison and likewise for males. Thus, male and female prevalence estimates are not directly comparable. * denotes that prevalence among sexual minority subgroup statistically significantly differs (at $p < 0.05$) from the prevalence among the heterosexual group of the same sex using bivariate logistic regression analysis.

Figure 2.2 shows age-adjusted prevalence estimates for health care access and affordability outcomes for transgender and cisgender veterans. We observed the following significant group differences:

- Transgender veterans were nearly twice as likely to report being unable to afford medical care during the past year as their cisgender veteran peers.

FIGURE 2.2

Health Care Access and Affordability Among Veterans, by Gender Identity

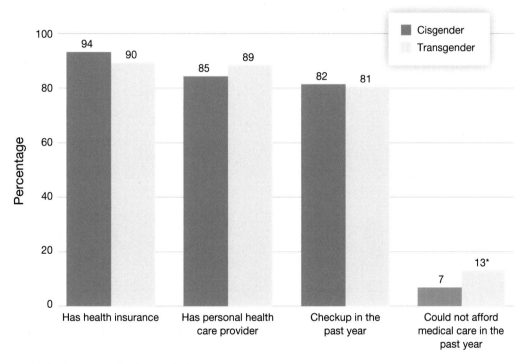

SOURCE: Uses BRFSS data from 2015–2021.

NOTE: Prevalence estimates among transgender veterans are age-standardized to the cisgender veterans group for comparison. * denotes that prevalence among the transgender veterans group statistically significantly differs (at $p < 0.05$) from the prevalence among the cisgender group using bivariate logistic regression analysis.

General Health Status

Figure 2.3 shows age-adjusted prevalence estimates for general health status outcomes (subjective overall health rated very good or excellent, exercise in past 30 days, and BMI between 18.5 and 25 [normal range]) for female and male veterans. The following significant group differences emerged:

- Bisexual male veterans and both male and female veterans with other sexual identities were less likely to report their overall health as "excellent" or "very good" than their heterosexual peers.
- Male veterans with other sexual identities were less likely to report exercising in the past month than heterosexual male veterans.
- Bisexual female veterans were less likely to have a BMI in the normal range (i.e., between 18.5 and 25) than heterosexual female veterans.
- Both gay male veterans and male veterans with other sexual identities were more likely to have a BMI in the normal range than heterosexual male veterans.

FIGURE 2.3

General Health Status Among Female and Male Veterans, by Sexual Identity

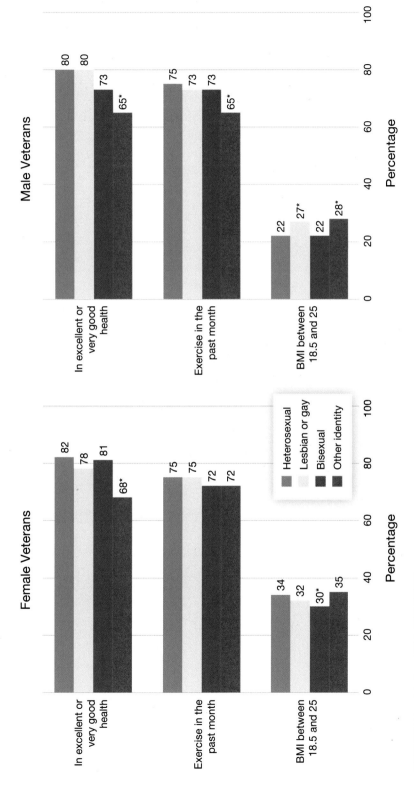

SOURCE: Uses data from 2015–2021 BRFSS.

NOTE: Prevalence estimates among female sexual minority groups are age-standardized to the female heterosexual group for comparison and likewise for males. Thus, male and female prevalence estimates are not directly comparable. * denotes that prevalence among sexual minority subgroup statistically significantly differs (at $p < 0.05$) from the prevalence among the heterosexual group of the same sex using bivariate logistic regression analysis.

Figure 2.4 shows age-adjusted prevalence estimates for indicators of past-month poor subjective physical health, poor subjective mental health, and functional impairment for female and male veterans. The following significant group differences emerged:

- Among female veterans, all sexual minority groups were more likely to report functional impairment (i.e., their health interfered with daily activities for more than two weeks during the past month) than heterosexual female veterans. Female veterans with other sexual identities were more than twice as likely to report functional impairment. Male veterans with other sexual identities were more likely to report functional impairment than heterosexual male veterans.
- Among both female and male veterans, all sexual minority groups were more likely to rate their mental health as "not good" for more than two weeks in the past month than their heterosexual peers., Both female and male veterans with other sexual identities were twice as likely to report poor mental health.
- Female veterans with other sexual identities were nearly twice as likely to rate their physical health as "not good" for greater than 2 weeks in the past month than heterosexual female veterans. Bisexual male veterans and male veterans with other sexual identities were more likely to report poor physical health than heterosexual male veterans.

FIGURE 2.4

Physical Health, Mental Health, and Functional Impairment Among Female and Male Veterans, by Sexual Identity

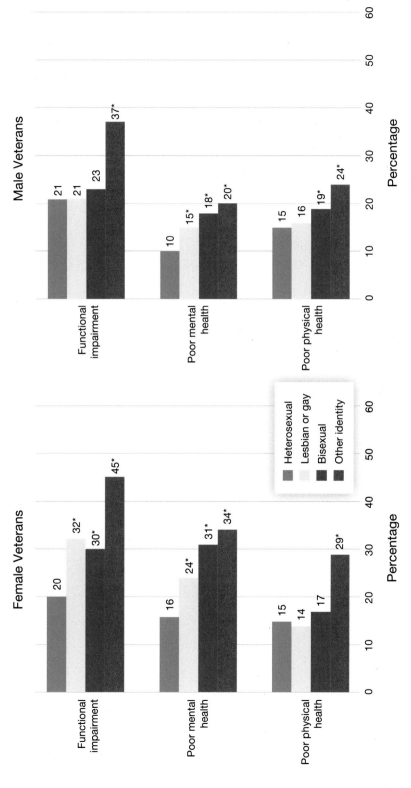

SOURCE: Uses data from 2015–2021 BRFSS.

NOTE: Prevalence estimates among female sexual minority groups are age-standardized to the female heterosexual group for comparison and likewise for males. Thus, male and female prevalence estimates are not directly comparable. * denotes that prevalence among sexual minority subgroup statistically significantly differs (at $p < 0.05$) from the prevalence among the heterosexual group of the same sex using bivariate logistic regression analysis.

Figure 2.5 shows age-adjusted prevalence estimates for general health status outcomes (subjective overall health rated *very good* or *excellent*, exercise in the past 30 days, and BMI in normal range) for transgender and cisgender veterans. The following significant group differences emerged:

- Transgender veterans were less likely to report their overall health as "excellent" or "very good" than cisgender veterans.
- Transgender veterans were less likely to report any exercise in the past month than cisgender veterans.
- Transgender veterans were more likely to have a BMI in the normal range than cisgender veterans.

FIGURE 2.5

General Health Status Among Veterans, by Gender Identity

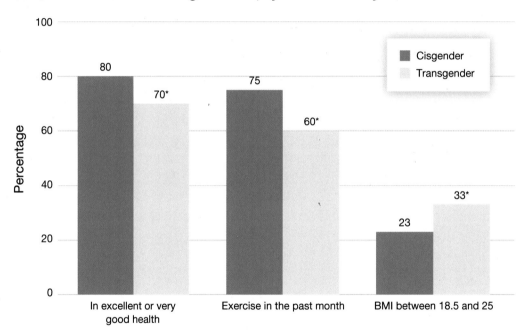

SOURCE: Uses data from 2015–2021 BRFSS.
NOTE: Prevalence estimates among transgender veterans are age-standardized to the cisgender veterans group for comparison. * denotes that prevalence among the transgender veterans group statistically significantly differs (at $p < 0.05$) from the prevalence among the cisgender group using bivariate logistic regression analysis.

Figure 2.6 shows age-adjusted prevalence estimates for indicators of past-month poor subjective physical health, poor subjective mental health, and functional impairment for transgender and cisgender veterans. The following significant group differences emerged:

- Transgender veterans were more likely to report functional impairment (i.e., their health interfered with daily activities for more than two weeks during the past month) than cisgender veterans.
- Transgender veterans were nearly twice as likely to rate their mental health as "not good" for more than two weeks in the past month than cisgender veterans.
- Transgender veterans were more likely to rate their physical health as "not good" for more than two weeks in the past month than cisgender veterans.

FIGURE 2.6

Physical Health, Mental Health, and Functional Impairment Among Veterans, by Gender Identity

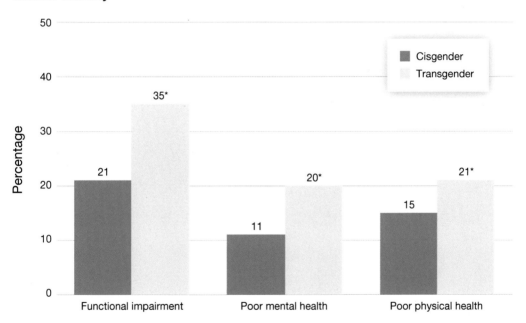

SOURCE: Uses data from 2015–2021 BRFSS.
NOTE: Prevalence estimates among transgender veterans are age-standardized to the cisgender veterans group for comparison. * denotes that prevalence among the transgender veterans group statistically significantly differs (at $p < 0.05$) from the prevalence among the cisgender group using bivariate logistic regression analysis.

Substance Use

Figure 2.7 shows age-adjusted prevalence estimates for alcohol use-related outcomes (any past-month alcohol use, binge drinking, or heavy consumption) for female and male veterans. The following significant group differences emerged:

- Lesbian or gay female veterans and bisexual female veterans were more likely to report any alcohol use in the past month than heterosexual female veterans.
- Male veterans with other sexual identities were less likely to report any alcohol use than heterosexual male veterans.
- Among female veterans, all sexual minority groups were more likely to report past-month binge drinking relative to heterosexual female veterans. The prevalence of binge drinking was nearly twice as high among bisexual female veterans and female veterans with other identities as that among heterosexual female veterans. Gay male veterans were more likely to report binge drinking than heterosexual male veterans.
- The prevalence of heavy alcohol consumption (more than seven drinks per week for women) was more than twice as high among lesbian or gay female veterans and four times as high among bisexual female veterans as that among heterosexual female veterans. Male veterans with other sexual identities were also more likely to report heavy alcohol consumption (more than 14 drinks per week for men) than heterosexual male veterans.

FIGURE 2.7

Alcohol Use Outcomes Among Female and Male Veterans, by Sexual Identity

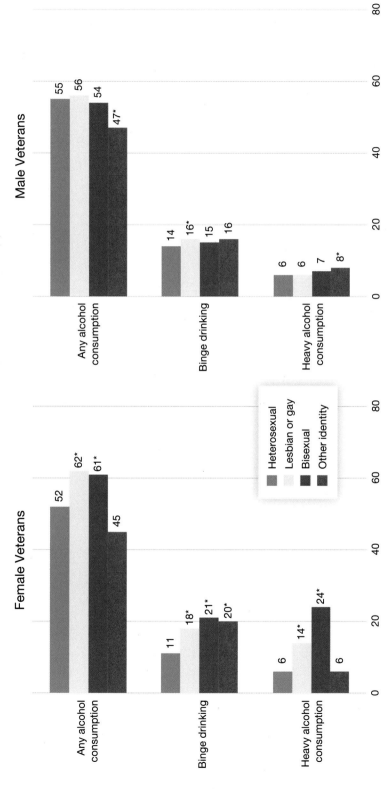

SOURCE: Uses data from 2015–2021 BRFSS.

NOTE: Prevalence estimates among female sexual minority groups are age-standardized to the female heterosexual group for comparison, and likewise for males. Thus, male and female prevalence estimates are not directly comparable. * denotes that prevalence among sexual minority subgroup statistically significantly differs (at $p < 0.05$) from the prevalence among the heterosexual group of the same sex using bivariate logistic regression analysis.

Figure 2.8 shows age-adjusted prevalence estimates for current (past-month) cigarette smoking for female and male veterans. The following significant group differences emerged:

- Lesbian or gay female veterans were nearly twice as likely to be current smokers than heterosexual female veterans.
- Gay male veterans were more likely to be current smokers than heterosexual male veterans.

FIGURE 2.8

Current Smoking Prevalence Among Female and Male Veterans, by Sexual Identity

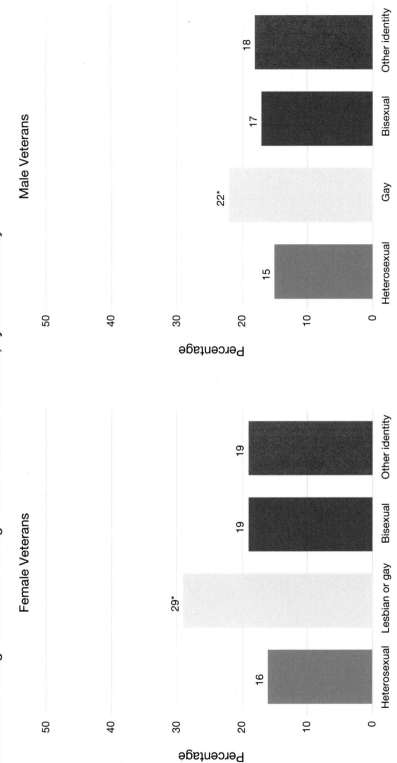

SOURCE: Uses data from 2015–2021 BRFSS.

NOTE: Prevalence estimates among female sexual minority groups are age-standardized to the female heterosexual group for comparison, and likewise for males. Thus, male and female prevalence estimates are not directly comparable. * denotes that prevalence among sexual minority subgroup statistically significantly differs (at $p < 0.05$) from the prevalence among the heterosexual group of the same sex using bivariate logistic regression analysis.

Figure 2.9 shows age-adjusted prevalence estimates for alcohol use-related outcomes for transgender and cisgender veterans. The following significant group difference emerged:

- Transgender veterans were less likely to have to report any alcohol use in the past month than cisgender veterans.

FIGURE 2.9

Alcohol Use Outcomes Among Veterans, by Gender Identity

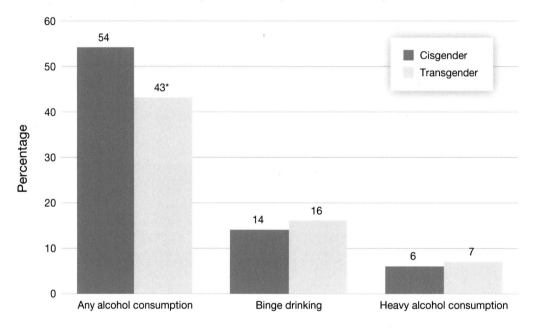

SOURCE: Uses data from 2015–2021 BRFSS.

NOTE: Prevalence estimates among transgender veterans are age-standardized to the cisgender veterans group for comparison. * denotes that prevalence among the transgender veterans group statistically significantly differs (at $p < 0.05$) from the prevalence among the cisgender group using bivariate logistic regression analysis.

Figure 2.10 shows age-adjusted prevalence estimates for current (past-month) cigarette smoking prevalence for transgender and cisgender veterans. The following significant group difference emerged:

- Transgender veterans were more likely to currently smoke cigarettes than cisgender veterans.

FIGURE 2.10

Current Smoking Among Veterans, by Gender Identity

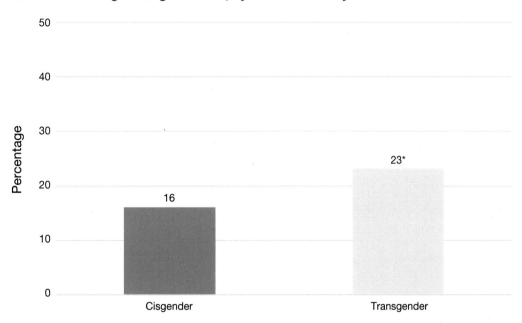

SOURCE: Uses data from 2015–2021 BRFSS.
NOTE: Prevalence estimates among transgender veterans are age-standardized to the cisgender veterans group for comparison. * denotes that prevalence among the transgender veterans group statistically significantly differs (at $p < 0.05$) from the prevalence among the cisgender group using bivariate logistic regression analysis

Chronic Health Conditions

Figure 2.11 shows age-adjusted prevalence estimates for cardiovascular disease-related outcomes (i.e., previously diagnosed with stroke, heart attack, or angina or CHD) for female and male veterans. The following significant group differences emerged:

- Among male veterans, individuals from all sexual minority groups were more likely to have had strokes than heterosexual male veterans. Specifically, prevalence of stroke was more than twice as high among male veterans with other sexual identities.
- Bisexual female veterans and female veterans with other sexual identities were more than twice as likely to have had a heart attack as heterosexual female veterans. Having a history of heart attack was also higher among bisexual male veterans and male veterans with other sexual identities than among heterosexual male veterans.
- Lesbian or gay female veterans and bisexual female veterans were more likely to have been diagnosed with angina or CHD than heterosexual female veterans. Specifically, the prevalence of angina or CHD was more than twice as high among lesbian or gay female veterans. Gay male veterans and male veterans with other sexual identities were more likely to have been diagnosed with angina or CHD than heterosexual male veterans.

FIGURE 2.11
Lifetime Prevalence of Cardiovascular Conditions Among Female and Male Veterans, by Sexual Identity

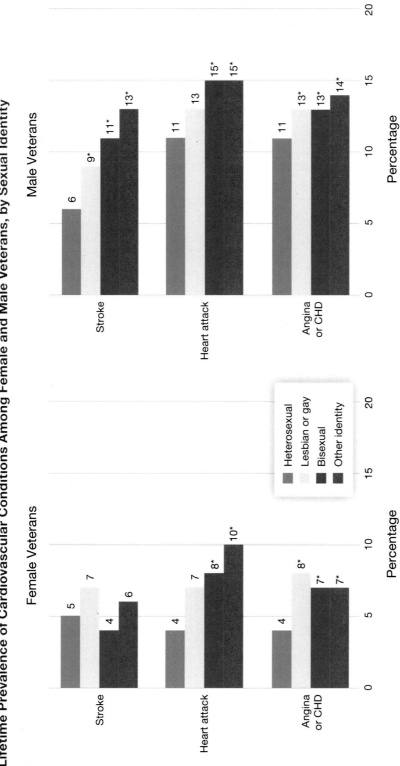

SOURCE: Uses data from 2015–2021 BRFSS.

NOTE: Prevalence estimates among female sexual minority groups are age-standardized to the female heterosexual group for comparison, and likewise for males. Thus, male and female prevalence estimates are not directly comparable. * denotes that prevalence among sexual minority subgroup statistically significantly differs (at $p < 0.05$) from the prevalence among the heterosexual group of the same sex using bivariate logistic regression analysis.

Figure 2.12 shows age-adjusted prevalence estimates for self-reported diagnosis of a depressive disorder for female and male veterans. The following significant group differences emerged:

- Among female veterans, individuals in all sexual minority groups were more likely to have been diagnosed with a depressive disorder than heterosexual female veterans. Bisexual female veterans were nearly twice as likely to have a lifetime depressive disorder diagnosis relative to heterosexual female veterans.
- Among male veterans, those from all sexual minority groups were more likely to have been diagnosed with a depressive disorder than heterosexual male veterans. Bisexual male veterans were nearly twice as likely to have a lifetime depressive disorder diagnosis relative to heterosexual male veterans.

FIGURE 2.12

Prevalence of Lifetime Depressive Disorder Among Female and Male Veterans, by Sexual Identity

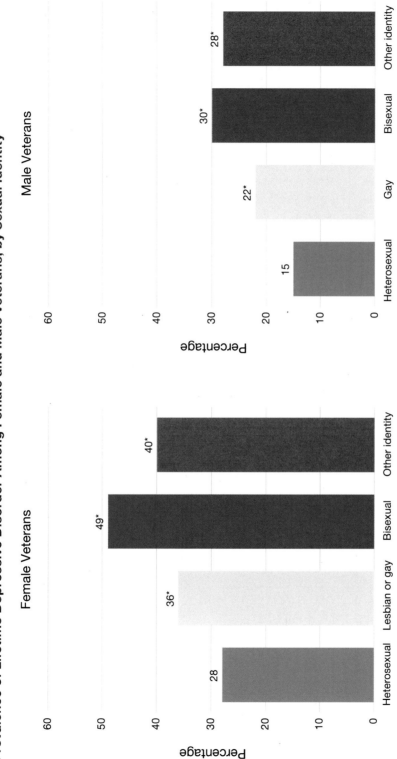

SOURCE: Uses data from 2015–2021 BRFSS.

NOTE: Prevalence estimates among female sexual minority groups are age-standardized to the female heterosexual group for comparison and likewise for males. Thus, male and female prevalence estimates are not directly comparable. * denotes that prevalence among sexual minority subgroup statistically significantly differs (at p < 0.05) from the prevalence among the heterosexual group of the same sex using bivariate logistic regression analysis.

Figure 2.13 shows age-adjusted prevalence estimates for lifetime diagnoses of other chronic health conditions for female veterans. The following significant group differences emerged:

- Lesbian or gay female veterans were more likely to have a lifetime diagnosis of arthritis, rheumatoid arthritis, gout, lupus, or fibromyalgia than heterosexual female veterans.
- All individuals from female sexual minority groups were more likely than heterosexual female veterans to have a lifetime diagnosis of COPD, emphysema, or chronic bronchitis. The prevalence of COPD, emphysema, or chronic bronchitis was three times higher among bisexual female veterans.
- Lesbian or gay female veterans and bisexual female veterans were more likely to have a lifetime asthma diagnosis than heterosexual female veterans; female veterans with other sexual identities were less likely to have a lifetime asthma diagnosis.
- Lesbian or gay female veterans and female veterans with other sexual identities were significantly more likely to report lifetime history of skin cancer diagnosis than heterosexual female veterans. Specifically, the prevalence of skin cancer was twice as high among female veterans with other sexual identities.
- Lesbian or gay female veterans were more likely to have been diagnosed with diabetes than heterosexual female veterans.

FIGURE 2.13

Lifetime Prevalence of Other Chronic Conditions Among Female Veterans, by Sexual Identity

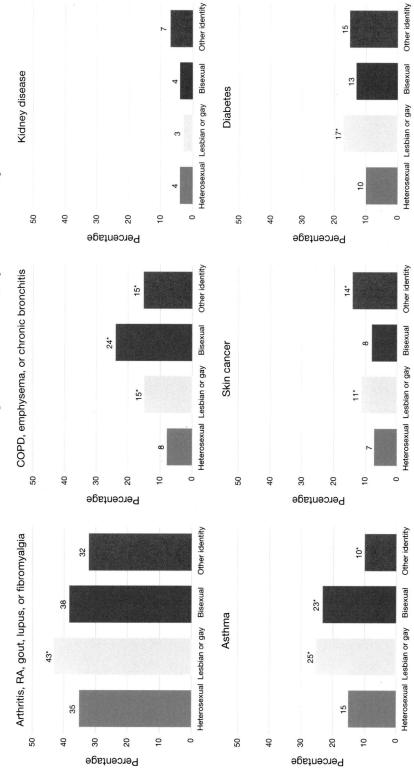

SOURCE: Uses data from 2015–2021 BRFSS.

NOTE: * denotes that prevalence among sexual minority subgroup statistically significantly differs (at $p < 0.05$) from the prevalence among the female heterosexual group using bivariate logistic regression analysis. RA = rheumatoid arthritis.

Figure 2.14 shows age-adjusted prevalence estimates for lifetime diagnoses of other chronic health conditions for male veterans. The following significant group differences emerged:

- Bisexual male veterans were more likely to have a lifetime diagnosis of arthritis, rheumatoid arthritis, gout, lupus, or fibromyalgia than heterosexual male veterans.
- All male individuals from sexual minority groups were more likely than heterosexual male veterans to report a lifetime diagnosis of COPD, emphysema, or chronic bronchitis. The prevalence of COPD, emphysema, or chronic bronchitis was nearly twice as high among bisexual male veterans.
- Bisexual male veterans were more likely to have a lifetime diagnosis of kidney disease than heterosexual male veterans.
- All male individuals from sexual minority groups were significantly more likely to have a lifetime diagnosis of asthma than heterosexual male veterans.
- Gay male veterans and bisexual male veterans were more likely to have been diagnosed with diabetes than heterosexual male veterans.

FIGURE 2.14

Lifetime Prevalence of Other Chronic Conditions Among Male Veterans, by Sexual Identity

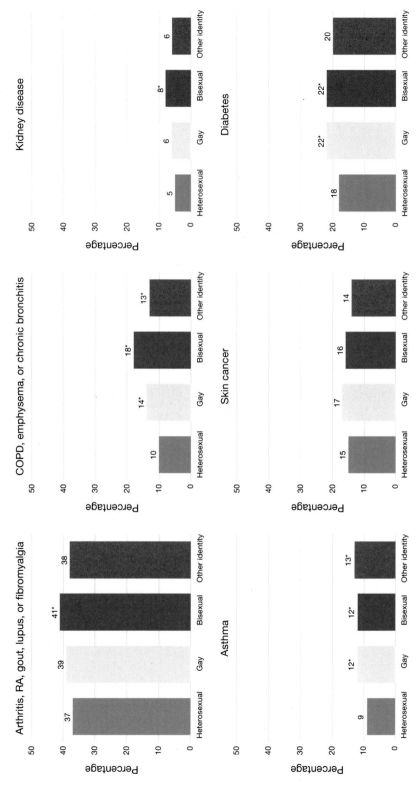

SOURCE: Uses data from 2015–2021 BRFSS.

NOTE: * denotes that prevalence among sexual minority subgroup statistically significantly differs (at $p < 0.05$) from the prevalence among the male heterosexual group using bivariate logistic regression analysis. RA = rheumatoid arthritis.

Figure 2.15 shows age-adjusted prevalence estimates for cardiovascular disease–related outcomes for transgender and cisgender veterans. The following significant group differences emerged:

- The lifetime prevalence of stroke was three times higher among transgender veterans than cisgender veterans.
- The lifetime prevalence of heart attack was more than twice as high among transgender veterans than cisgender veterans.
- The lifetime prevalence of angina or CHD was more than twice as high among transgender veterans than cisgender veterans.

FIGURE 2.15

Lifetime Prevalence of Cardiovascular Conditions Among Veterans, by Gender Identity

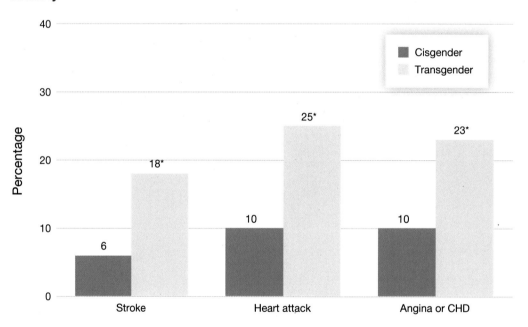

SOURCE: Uses data from 2015–2021 BRFSS.
NOTE: Prevalence estimates among transgender veterans are age-standardized to the cisgender veterans group for comparison. * denotes that prevalence among the transgender veterans group statistically significantly differs (at $p < 0.05$) from the prevalence among the cisgender group using bivariate logistic regression analysis.

Figure 2.16 shows age-adjusted prevalence estimates for lifetime depressive disorder diagnoses for transgender and cisgender veterans. The following significant group difference emerged:

- Transgender veterans were twice as likely to have a lifetime diagnosis of depressive disorder as cisgender veterans.

FIGURE 2.16

Prevalence of Lifetime Depressive Disorder Among Veterans, by Gender Identity

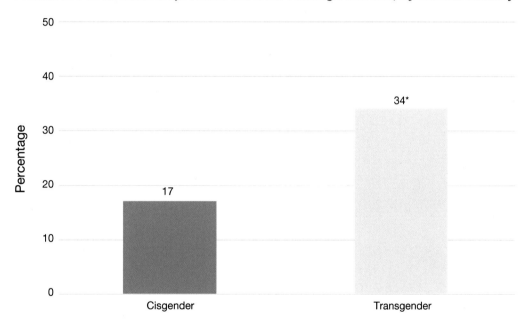

SOURCE: Uses data from 2015–2021 BRFSS.

NOTE: Prevalence estimates among transgender veterans are age-standardized to the cisgender veterans group for comparison. * denotes that prevalence among the transgender veterans group statistically significantly differs (at $p < 0.05$) from the prevalence among the cisgender group using bivariate logistic regression analysis.

Figure 2.17 shows age-adjusted prevalence estimates for other chronic health conditions for transgender and cisgender veterans. The following significant group differences emerged:

- The lifetime prevalence of arthritis, rheumatoid arthritis, gout, lupus, or fibromyalgia was higher among transgender veterans than cisgender veterans.
- The lifetime prevalence of COPD, emphysema, or chronic bronchitis was more than twice as high among transgender veterans than cisgender veterans.
- The lifetime kidney disease prevalence was three times higher among transgender veterans than among cisgender veterans.
- Transgender veterans were twice as likely to report a lifetime asthma diagnosis than cisgender veterans.
- Transgender veterans were twice as likely to report a lifetime skin cancer diagnosis than cisgender veterans.
- Transgender veterans were more likely to report a lifetime diabetes diagnosis than cisgender veterans.

FIGURE 2.17

Lifetime Prevalence of Other Chronic Conditions Among Veterans, by Gender Identity

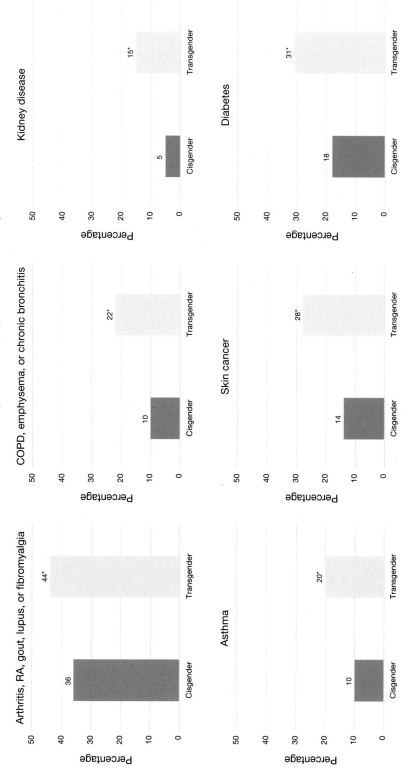

SOURCE: Uses data from 2015–2021 BRFSS.

NOTE: Prevalence estimates among transgender veterans are age-standardized to the cisgender veterans group for comparison. * denotes that prevalence among the transgender veterans group statistically significantly differs (at $p < 0.05$) from the prevalence among the cisgender group using bivariate logistic regression analysis. RA = rheumatoid arthritis.

CHAPTER 3

Summary of Differences in Health-Related Outcomes, by Sexual and Gender Identity

To summarize findings across all the analyses presented in Chapter 2, Table 3.1 shows whether there was a difference between the sexual or gender minority group and the reference heterosexual or cisgender group indicates for each outcome. A *worse* in a red-shaded cell indicates that the outcome was significantly worse for the sexual or gender identity group than for the heterosexual or cisgender comparison group, and a *better* in a green-shaded cell indicates that the outcome was significantly better for the sexual or gender identity group than for the heterosexual or cisgender comparison group. Unshaded cells with "ND" indicate that there was no significant difference between groups.

As illustrated in the table, group differences were observed for all outcomes examined. In most—but not all—instances, sexual minority veterans had poorer outcomes than same-sex heterosexual veterans. Similarly, transgender veterans showed poorer outcomes than cisgender veterans on 17 of the 24 outcomes examined. However, specific patterns of differences varied slightly across groups and outcome domains. For example, lesbian or gay female veterans did not differ from heterosexual female veterans with respect to health care access and affordability outcomes, whereas bisexual female veterans showed poorer outcomes than heterosexual female veterans for three of four outcomes in this domain (checkup in past year, insurance status, and health care affordability). Additionally, transgender veterans were more likely than cisgender veterans to have a BMI between 18 and 25 (in the normal range) but showed poorer outcomes than cisgender veterans for all outcomes in the chronic health conditions domain.

TABLE 3.1

Summary of Differences in Health-Related Outcomes, by Sexual and Gender Identity Groups

Health-Related Outcome	Females (ref: Heterosexual)			Males (ref: Heterosexual)			Transgender (ref: Cisgender)
	Lesbian or Gay	Bisexual	Other Sexual Identity	Gay	Bisexual	Other Sexual Identity	
Health care access and affordability							
Has health insurance	ND	worse	ND	ND	worse	ND	ND
Has personal health care provider	ND	ND	ND	ND	ND	ND	ND
Had checkup in past year	ND	worse	ND	ND	ND	ND	ND
Could not afford medical care, past year	ND	worse	worse	worse	worse	worse	worse
General health status							
Self-reported health is excellent or very good	ND	ND	worse	ND	worse	worse	worse
Exercise in the past month	ND	ND	ND	ND	ND	worse	worse
BMI between 18.5 and 25 (normal range)	ND	worse	ND	better	ND	better	better
Functional impairment	worse	worse	worse	ND	worse	worse	worse
Mental health not good 14+ days in the past month	worse	worse	worse	worse	worse	worse	worse
Physical health not good 14+ days in the past month	ND	ND	worse	ND	worse	worse	worse
Substance use							
Cigarette smoking	worse	ND	ND	worse	ND	ND	worse
Any alcohol use	worse	worse	ND	ND	ND	better	better
Binge drinking	worse	worse	worse	worse	ND	ND	ND
Heavy alcohol use	worse	worse	ND	ND	ND	worse	ND

Table 3.1—Continued

Health-Related Outcome	Females (ref: Heterosexual)			Males (ref: Heterosexual)			Transgender (ref: Cisgender)
	Lesbian or Gay	Bisexual	Other Sexual Identity	Gay	Bisexual	Other Sexual Identity	
Chronic health conditions (Ever told you had:)							
Angina or CHD	worse	worse	ND	worse	ND	worse	worse
Heart attack	ND	worse	worse	ND	worse	worse	worse
Stroke	ND	ND	ND	worse	worse	worse	worse
Depressive disorder	worse	worse	worse	worse	worse	worse	worse
Diabetes	worse	ND	ND	worse	worse	ND	worse
Kidney disease	ND	ND	ND	ND	worse	ND	worse
Arthritis, rheumatoid arthritis, gout, lupus, or fibromyalgia	worse	worse	worse	ND	worse	ND	worse
COPD, emphysema, or chronic bronchitis	worse	worse	worse	worse	worse	worse	worse
Asthma	worse	worse	worse	worse	worse	worse	worse
Skin cancer	worse	worse	worse	ND	ND	ND	worse

SOURCE: Uses data from 2015–2021 BRFSS data.

NOTE: ND = no significant difference relative to reference group. Red shading indicates a statistically significant difference in the less favorable direction relative to the reference group. Green shading indicates a statistically significant difference in the more favorable direction relative to the reference group.

43

Associations Between State Policy Climate in 2015 and Health-Related Outcomes Among LGBTQ+ Veterans

Table 4.1 shows adjusted odds ratios from separate logistic regression models examining associations between 2015 state LGBTQ+ policy climate and health outcomes in 2015–2017 BRFSS data among LGBTQ+ veterans. As shown in the table, compared with those living in states with negative 2015 MAP policy ratings, respondents living in states with more favorable LGBTQ+ policy climates (low, medium, or high categories) generally showed more-favorable outcomes for some health-related variables of focus:

- State LGBTQ+ policy climate was associated with some indications of health care access.
  - Having a more-favorable LGBTQ+ policy climate was associated with health insurance status, such that individuals residing in states with better state policy ratings (low, medium, or high) were significantly more likely to report having health insurance and having had a check-up visit with a health care provider in the past year compared with LGBTQ+ veterans residing in states with a negative LGBTQ+ policy climate.
  - Individuals in states with high policy ratings were more likely to report having a personal health care provider than those in states with negative ratings.
  - LGBTQ+ veterans residing in states with medium policy climates were also less likely to report that they could not afford care in the past year than individuals in states with negative policy climates.
- We observed few statistically significant associations between state LGBTQ+ policy climate and outcomes in other domains. Where significant associations were observed, findings generally indicated better outcomes for individuals in states with more favorable (compared with negative) policy climates, with one exception.
  - Individuals residing in states with low, medium, or high policy ratings were less likely to report current cigarette smoking than those in states with negative LGBTQ+ policy ratings in 2015.

- Compared with individuals residing in states with a negative climate, those in states with low policy climates in 2015 were also less likely to report that their mental health had not been good for two or more weeks in the past month.
- Individuals in states with medium policy climates were less likely to report having a history of COPD or a related condition than individuals residing in states with a negative policy climate.
- LGBTQ+ veterans residing in states with medium policy climates were more likely than those in states with negative policy climates to report having a lifetime history of angina or CHD.

TABLE 4.1

Associations Between 2015 State LGBTQ+ Policy Rating and Health-Related Outcomes Among LGBTQ+ Veterans, 2015–2017

Health Outcome	LGBTQ+ State Policy Climate in 2015 (reference category: Negative)		
	Low	Medium	High
	OR (95% CI)	OR (95% CI)	OR (95% CI)
Health care access			
Has health insurance	**2.99 (1.19,7.51)**	**2.86 (1.26,6.47)**	**4.68 (2.18,10.07)**
Has a personal health care provider	1.05 (0.54,2.04)	1.07 (0.54,2.11)	**2.10 (1.12,3.96)**
Had checkup in past year	**2.40 (1.28,4.49)**	**2.42 (1.36,4.32)**	**2.07 (1.17,3.65)**
Could not afford medical care in the past 12 months	0.60 (0.32,1.13)	**0.44 (0.22,0.88)**	0.64 (0.32,1.26)
General health status and health behaviors			
Self-reported health is excellent or very good	1.36 (0.79,2.37)	1.08 (0.65,1.79)	1.13 (0.70,1.83)
Exercise in past 30 days	1.54 (0.90,2.62)	1.10 (0.68,1.79)	1.52 (0.92,2.51)
BMI between 18.5 and 25 (normal range)	0.98 (0.58,1.64)	0.94 (0.57,1.55)	1.18 (0.75,1.87)
Physical health not good for 14+ days in the past month	1.15 (0.56,2.35)	1.11 (0.52,2.38)	1.08 (0.57,2.06)
Mental health not good for 14+ days in the past month	**0.44 (0.21,0.89)**	0.83 (0.41,1.66)	0.73 (0.36,1.49)
Functional impairments (health interfered with daily activities for 14+ days in the past month)	0.98 (0.50,1.92)	0.98 (0.46,2.07)	1.00 (0.54,1.86)

Table 4.1—Continued

Health Outcome	LGBTQ+ State Policy Climate in 2015 (reference category: Negative)		
	Low	Medium	High
	OR (95% CI)	OR (95% CI)	OR (95% CI)
Substance use			
Current smoking	**0.43 (0.25,0.74)**	**0.48 (0.28,0.81)**	**0.35 (0.20,0.60)**
Drank any alcoholic beverages in the past 30 days	1.03 (0.65,1.65)	1.08 (0.70,1.66)	1.29 (0.85,1.96)
Binge drinking in the past 30 days	0.59 (0.31,1.11)	0.66 (0.38,1.15)	0.67 (0.38,1.19)
Heavy alcohol consumption in the past 30 days	0.75 (0.30,1.89)	0.80 (0.37,1.76)	0.53 (0.22,1.31)
Chronic health conditions			
Lifetime angina or CHD	1.11 (0.47,2.59)	**2.34 (1.13,4.84)**	1.30 (0.67,2.49)
Lifetime heart attack	0.71 (0.33,1.54)	1.00 (0.46,2.17)	1.16 (0.62,2.16)
Lifetime stroke	0.55 (0.21,1.47)	0.61 (0.27,1.38)	1.62 (0.79,3.35)
Lifetime depressive disorder	0.89 (0.53,1.51)	0.79 (0.48,1.30)	1.13 (0.70,1.81)
Lifetime diabetes	1.19 (0.66,2.15)	1.00 (0.57,1.75)	1.00 (0.59,1.71)
Lifetime kidney disease	1.40 (0.58,3.37)	1.61 (0.60,4.33)	0.83 (0.35,1.95)
Lifetime arthritis, rheumatoid arthritis, gout, lupus, or fibromyalgia	1.04 (0.63,1.71)	0.77 (0.47,1.25)	0.86 (0.53,1.37)
Lifetime COPD, emphysema, or chronic bronchitis	0.75 (0.41,1.39)	**0.50 (0.26,0.97)**	0.91 (0.49,1.68)
Lifetime asthma	0.64 (0.32,1.28)	0.69 (0.35,1.35)	1.12 (0.59,2.13)
Lifetime skin cancer	1.79 (0.91,3.51)	0.65 (0.29,1.47)	1.13 (0.56,2.29)

SOURCE: Uses data from 2015–2017 BRFSS and state policy tallies from MAP, 2015.
NOTE: CI = confidence interval; OR = odds ratio. Estimates are adjusted odds ratios from separate multiple logistic regression analyses examining associations between 2015 state LGBTQ+ policy category (negative [reference category], low, medium, or high) and each dichotomous health-related outcome. All models controlled for survey year, age, race and ethnicity, sex, and education. Bolded text indicates a statistically significant difference (from negative state policy category) at $p < 0.05$.

CHAPTER 5

Conclusions and Recommendations

In this report, we use a large representative sample to characterize differences in health status and access to health care for sexual and gender minority veterans (relative to their heterosexual and cisgender veteran peers) and examine differences in health-related outcomes for LGBTQ+ veterans by state LGBTQ+ policy climate. We address key gaps in the existing literature on health disparities and heterogeneity in LGBTQ+ veterans' health and well-being.

We observe significant differences related to sexual or gender identity for all outcomes that we examined: Nearly all significant differences indicated worse outcomes for sexual and gender minorities compared with their heterosexual or cisgender peers. These findings align with prior research of both the general population and service members and veterans that indicates significant disparities with respect to health care access and well-being for LGBTQ+ individuals relative to cisgender and heterosexual peers (Carey et al., 2022; Kondo et al., 2017; Mark et al., 2019; Murphy et al., 2023; Patterson, Sepúlveda, and White, 2020). Findings significantly extend previous work by demonstrating that such disparities are evident across multiple domains, including health care access, general health status, substance use, and history of specific chronic conditions.

Some differences in outcomes observed in this study were consistent across all sexual and gender minority groups examined, when compared with their heterosexual and cisgender peers, including mental health outcomes (e.g., subjective mental health, lifetime history of depression) and some chronic physical health conditions (e.g., chronic respiratory disease, asthma). However, there was also heterogeneity with respect to consistency with which differences were observed for specific identity groups (e.g., bisexual women compared with heterosexual women) across multiple outcomes. Additionally, there are many cases in which the pattern of differences across sexual identity groups compared with their heterosexual peers differed between females and males. For instance, rates of alcohol use, binge drinking, and heavy alcohol consumption are all higher among bisexual women than among heterosexual women, but these outcomes are not higher among bisexual men compared with heterosexual men. A similar example is BMI; bisexual females are less likely to have a BMI in the normal range than heterosexual females, while gay and other sexual identity men are more likely to have a BMI in the normal range than heterosexual men. Such findings are consistent with data indicating that LGBTQ+ individuals are not a monolith (Committee on Lesbian, Gay, Bisexual and Transgender Health Issues and Research Gaps and Opportunities, 2011; Brown and Jones, 2014; Patterson, Sepúlveda, and White, 2020) and call attention to the importance of disaggregating by identity and other characteristics to understand how and for whom health-related disparities may manifest.

Two other general findings are notable. First, the consistency of findings showing poorer outcomes for transgender veterans compared with cisgender veterans is striking. Of the 24 outcomes examined, transgender veterans had significantly poorer outcomes than cisgender veterans on 17 outcomes, including measures of health-related functional impairment and subjective health, as well as clinically diagnosed conditions, such as CHD and diabetes. Second, many of the conditions that were more prevalent among sexual and gender minority veterans relative to their heterosexual and cisgender peers are outcomes of processes that occur over time, such as diabetes or stroke, suggesting that the differences are likely the result of differences in health-related exposures (e.g., chronic stressors) that have accrued over a lifetime.

As a whole, these findings underscore the importance of ongoing efforts to reduce treatment gaps and address disparities in health and health care access for LGBTQ+ individuals. For example, compared with their heterosexual peers, bisexual female and male veterans were significantly less likely to report having health insurance. Additionally, some sexual minority veterans (e.g., bisexual men and women, gay men, men and women with other identities) and transgender veterans were more likely to report inability to afford medical care in the past year compared with their heterosexual and cisgender peers. This suggests that targeted efforts to enhance awareness of benefits and available services and ensure accessibility to low-cost health care may be needed to address disparities for these groups. For example, the U.S. Department of Defense's (DoD's) proactive efforts to review discharge records for individuals affected by DADT may help to ensure that veterans who were discharged under less-than-honorable conditions prior to DADT repeal are able to request corrections to their military records and take full advantage of the benefits for which they may be eligible (i.e., provided the original discharge was based solely on DADT or a similar policy and there are no additional aggravating factors in the discharge record) (DoD, undated). However, reports published in 2023 indicate that many veterans remain unaware of the process, experience lengthy and burdensome reviews, or both; such barriers have prompted a number of congresspersons to call for additional oversight and request DoD to review and improve this process to reduce burdens to veterans (Garcia, Pocan, and Pappas, 2024; Suter, 2024). In a letter to Secretary of Defense Lloyd Austin III on January 25, 2024, members of the U.S. House of Representatives Robert Garcia, Mark Pocan, and Chris Pappas emphasized that among the more than14,000 veterans separated under the "Homosexual Conduct" policy with less than honorable discharge between 1980 and DADT's repeal in 2011, "only 1,683 have applied to have their discharge upgraded . . . leaving a vast majority of less than honorable discharges under DADT and the preceding policy uncorrected." (Garcia, Pocan, and Pappas, 2024). Actions to expedite the review process, increase awareness for LGBTQ+ veterans and their families, and remove administrative barriers and potential costs (e.g., legal representation for applicants) for veterans affected by DADT may be needed.

Additional efforts, such as continued support for and expansion of LGBTQ+-affirming services within the VHA, might also be instrumental in reducing disparities for LGBTQ+

veterans and ensuring that individuals are aware of and can connect with available services in the VA system and in their communities. For example, all VA health care systems have an LGBTQ+ veteran care coordinator to assist veterans in connecting with a variety of health care and related services (U.S. Department of Veterans Affairs, undated). Ensuring that there is adequate continued support for and visibility of such resources for LGBTQ+ veterans may be instrumental in closing substantial gaps in care and reducing disparities for these individuals. Existing VHA policies stipulate that health care for LGBTQ+ veterans must be "delivered in an affirming and inclusive environment and that VHA employees respect" veterans' identities (U.S. Department of Veterans Affairs, undated; U.S. Department of Veterans Affairs Office of Resolution Management, Diversity, and Inclusion, 2022). In the context of the VA system, maintaining such policies and related employee training and communication efforts could be instrumental in mitigating known barriers to accessing health services for LGBTQ+ individuals, such as concerns related to stigma and mistreatment from care providers (Committee on Lesbian, Gay, Bisexual and Transgender Health Issues and Research Gaps and Opportunities, 2011; Grogan et al., 2020; James et al., 2016). These efforts may help to ensure that LGBTQ+ veterans feel comfortable accessing and are able to receive high quality, timely, and appropriate care.

Encouragingly, one 2019 survey of a small sample of LGBTQ+ veterans enrolled in VHA (n = 151) found that a majority of respondents reported largely positive experiences with VHA services and felt welcome and comfortable disclosing their identities to providers at VA facilities (Kauth, Barrera, and Latini, 2019). However, this same study also identified less positive experiences among some transgender respondents, which could signal a need for additional actions to ensure that gender-diverse veterans receive high-quality care in inclusive and affirming settings. Of note, although the VA announced plans to begin providing gender confirmation surgery in 2021, because of delays in the rulemaking process, those critical services are not yet available to transgender veterans who need them (Shane, 2024). This delay has prompted legal action from the Transgender American Veterans Association and Yale Law School's Veterans Legal Services Clinic, who filed a lawsuit against the Department of Veterans Affairs on January 25, 2024, to prompt action on moving forward with the provision of gender confirmation surgeries to VA patients. Efforts to finalize the rulemaking process as soon as possible will help to ensure that LGBTQ+ veterans are able to access necessary gender-affirming care in a timely manner. Unfortunately, calls to remove or weaken protections and availability of services for LGBTQ+ VA patients by, for example, prohibiting VA providers from providing medically necessary gender-affirming care (Shane, 2023) have the potential to exacerbate to disparities observed for LGBTQ+ veterans compared with their heterosexual and cisgender counterparts. More broadly, recent state- and local-level policy proposals targeting gender-affirming healthcare (i.e., not specific to veterans' services) could worsen disparities for gender-minority veterans and could hinder federal efforts to improve health and well-being for these individuals. Additional studies are urgently needed to assess the impact of more-recent changes in policy on health and related outcomes for LGBTQ+ veterans.

Among LGBTQ+ veterans, state LGBTQ+ policy climate was also associated with some health-related outcomes. Where significant associations were observed, a more-positive state LGBTQ+ policy climate was typically associated with better outcomes. For example, compared with individuals who resided in states with negative LGBTQ+ policy ratings in 2015, LGBTQ+ veterans living in states with more favorable policy climates (low, medium, or high) were more than twice as likely to report having health insurance and having had a check-up in the past year than those residing in states with negative LGBTQ+ policy climates. The lone exception to this pattern was the finding that individuals in states with medium policy climates were more likely than those in negative policy climate states to report lifetime history of angina or CHD. Although the reasons for this are unclear, one possibility is that individuals in states with more-favorable policy climates may be more likely to receive diagnosis and treatment for angina or CHD—consistent with findings indicating that there is greater health care accessibility in these groups than in those of their peers in negative policy states. Additionally, those living in states with low, medium, or high 2015 LGBTQ+ policy ratings were significantly less likely to report current cigarette smoking than individuals in states with negative ratings in 2015.

Collectively, these findings suggest that more-favorable state LGBTQ+ policy climate may correlate with better health-related outcomes in some domains for LGBTQ+ veterans. However, it is important to note that LGBTQ+ policies may also correlate with myriad other policy and related factors (e.g., state Medicaid expansion status, local- and state-level public health initiatives and prevention activities, health care provider shortages) that can affect health-related outcomes—particularly, constructs related to health care access (e.g., insurance status)—for LGBTQ+ individuals (Blosnich et al., 2016; Dawson, Kates, and Damico, 2018; Goldenberg et al., 2020; Tran et al., 2023). Future studies are needed to understand how the interplay of different policies may influence health-related outcomes for LGBTQ+ veterans. Moreover, LGBTQ+ policy climate is dynamic. Numerous states and localities have implemented or proposed new policies in the past decade (e.g., prohibiting insurance coverage or provision of gender-affirming health care) that may affect health and health care access for LGBTQ+ people (American Civil Liberties Union, 2024; MAP, 2024). Such actions may worsen disparities for sexual and gender minority veterans and could stymie federal efforts to improve health and well-being for these individuals. More studies are urgently needed to understand how changing LGBTQ+ policies over time could intersect with other factors at multiple levels (e.g., individual, interpersonal, community, policy, structural) to influence health-related outcomes for LGBTQ+ veterans.

As with all studies, these findings should be considered in the context of both strengths and limitations. First, our use of the large, representative BRFSS datasets provided a large effective sample size to examine prevalence estimates for a variety of health-related outcomes among sexual minority and gender-diverse veterans. However, our scope was limited to constructs available in the core BRFSS survey. For example, we were unable to examine factors relevant to characterizing disparities in health and service use, such as types of care accessed by respondents (e.g., preventative care, specialty mental health care, substance use treatment).

As stated in the "Data Sources and Measures" section in Chapter 1, the BRFSS sex variable likely is subject to measurement error both as a result of interviewers recording sex in 2015 (rather than asking respondents self-report) and because of potential conflation of biological sex and current gender identity because of the ambiguity of question wording. Furthermore, the BRFSS variable used to determine veteran status may have led to inclusion of some individuals who were on active duty or reserve. Additionally, as is the case with many studies, small cell sizes for transgender individuals precluded examination of subgroup differences for transgender individuals (e.g., trans men versus trans women versus nonbinary individuals, differences by sexual identity). Furthermore, we were unable to examine intersections between sexual identity, gender identity, and other important characteristics, such as race and ethnicity and socioeconomic status, that may affect health-related disparities. We did not adjust for multiple comparisons; although this does not affect the prevalence estimates presented in this report, adjustment for multiple comparisons may affect interpretation of statistical significance of some group differences. Finally, as noted previously, our use of 2015 MAP LGBTQ+ state policy ratings precluded analysis of how changes in LGBTQ+ policy climate over time may affect health-related outcomes for LGBTQ+ veterans.

With this study, we add to the growing body of literature indicating significant disparities in access to health care and health-related outcomes across multiple domains for sexual and gender minority veterans. Our findings underscore the importance and urgency of efforts to improve health services and outcomes for LGBTQ+ veterans, including actions to ensure that all LGBTQ+ veterans are able to use the benefits for which they are eligible and can access appropriate care when needed.

Prevalence Estimates and Tests of Group Differences, by Sexual Identity and Gender Identity

Tables A.1 through A.12 show age-adjusted prevalence estimates for veterans' health-related outcomes by sexual and gender identity groups in 2015–2021 BRFSS data. These tables also show results from logistic regression models that examined group differences in prevalence estimates for each outcome.

TABLE A.1

Health Care Access Among Female Veterans, by Sexual Identity: Age-Adjusted Prevalence Estimates and Odds Ratios

Health Care Access Outcome	Heterosexual Female — Reference Prevalence	Lesbian or Gay Female — Age-Adjusted Prevalence	Lesbian or Gay Female — OR (95% CI)	Bisexual Female — Age-Adjusted Prevalence	Bisexual Female — OR (95% CI)	Other Sexual Identity, Female — Age-Adjusted Prevalence	Other Sexual Identity, Female — OR (95% CI)
Has health insurance	94%	88%	0.94 (0.86, 1.02)	85%	**0.91 (0.83, 0.98)**	88%	0.94 (0.81, 1.06)
Has a personal health care provider	86%	84%	0.98 (0.89, 1.06)	81%	0.94 (0.86, 1.02)	85%	0.98 (0.85, 1.12)
Had checkup in past year	82%	78%	0.95 (0.86, 1.03)	68%	**0.82 (0.74, 0.9)**	72%	0.87 (0.74, 1)
Could not afford medical care in the past 12 months	11%	11%	1.03 (0.8, 1.27)	22%	**2.00 (1.69, 2.31)**	21%	**1.93 (1.41, 2.45)**

SOURCE: Uses data from 2015–2021 BRFSS.
NOTE: Prevalence estimates among female sexual minority groups are age-standardized to the female heterosexual group for comparison. Odds ratios are from separate logistic regression models comparing sexual identity group prevalence estimates (reference group: heterosexual veterans). Bolded text indicates significant difference from heterosexual group at $p < 0.05$.

TABLE A.2

Health Care Access Among Male Veterans, by Sexual Identity: Age-Adjusted Prevalence Estimates and Odds Ratios

Health Care Access Outcome	Heterosexual Male	Gay Male		Bisexual Male		Other Sexual Identity Male	
	Reference Prevalence	Age-Adjusted Prevalence	OR (95% CI)	Age-Adjusted Prevalence	OR (95% CI)	Age-Adjusted Prevalence	OR (95% CI)
Has health insurance	95%	92%	0.97 (0.92, 1.03)	90%	**0.95 (0.90, 1.00)**	92%	0.97 (0.9, 1.04)
Has a personal health care provider	85%	88%	1.04 (0.98, 1.1)	82%	0.97 (0.91, 1.02)	83%	0.98 (0.9, 1.05)
Had checkup in past year	82%	86%	1.05 (0.98, 1.11)	81%	0.98 (0.92, 1.04)	80%	0.97 (0.9, 1.04)
Could not afford medical care in the past 12 months	6%	10%	**1.56 (1.29, 1.83)**	12%	**1.90 (1.62, 2.17)**	13%	**2.09 (1.7, 2.48)**

SOURCE: Using data from the 2015–2021 BRFSS.
NOTE: Prevalence estimates among male sexual minority groups are age-standardized to the male heterosexual group for comparison. Odds ratios are from separate logistic regression models comparing sexual identity group prevalence estimates (reference group: heterosexual veterans). Bolded text indicates significant difference from heterosexual group at p < 0.05.

TABLE A.3

General Health Status and Health Behaviors Among Female Veterans, by Sexual Identity: Age-Adjusted Prevalence Estimates and Odds Ratios

Health Status and Behavior Outcome	Heterosexual Female	Lesbian or Gay Female		Bisexual Female		Other Sexual Identity Female	
	Reference Prevalence	Age-Adjusted Prevalence	OR (95% CI)	Age-Adjusted Prevalence	OR (95% CI)	Age-Adjusted Prevalence	OR (95% CI)
Self-reported health is excellent or very good	82%	78%	0.94 (0.86, 1.02)	81%	0.98 (0.9, 1.06)	68%	**0.82 (0.69, 0.95)**
Exercise in past 30 days	75%	75%	1.01 (0.92, 1.1)	72%	0.96 (0.88, 1.05)	72%	0.99 (0.84, 1.14)
BMI between 18.5 and 25 (normal range)	34%	32%	0.93 (0.8, 1.07)	30%	**0.86 (0.74, 0.98)**	35%	1.01 (0.77, 1.25)
Physical health not good for 14+ days in the past month	15%	14%	0.93 (0.71, 1.14)	17%	1.17 (0.92, 1.42)	29%	**1.95 (1.47, 2.44)**
Mental health not good for 14+ days in the past month	16%	24%	**1.50 (1.26, 1.74)**	31%	**1.89 (1.63, 2.14)**	34%	**2.06 (1.61, 2.52)**
Functional impairments (Health interfered with daily activities for 14+ days in the past month)	20%	32%	**1.64 (1.34, 1.94)**	30%	**1.52 (1.27, 1.78)**	45%	**2.28 (1.75, 2.82)**

SOURCE: Uses data from 2015–2021 BRFSS.

NOTE: Prevalence estimates among female sexual minority groups are age-standardized to the female heterosexual group for comparison. Odds ratios are from separate logistic regression models comparing sexual identity group prevalence estimates (reference group: heterosexual veterans). Bolded text indicates significant difference from heterosexual group at $p < 0.05$.

TABLE A.4

General Health Status and Health Behaviors Among Male Veterans, by Sexual Identity: Age-Adjusted Prevalence Estimates and Odds Ratios

Health Status and Behavior Outcome	Heterosexual Male	Gay Male		Bisexual Male		Other Sexual Identity Male	
	Reference Prevalence	Age-Adjusted Prevalence	OR (95% CI)	Age-Adjusted Prevalence	OR (95% CI)	Age-Adjusted Prevalence	OR (95% CI)
Self-reported health is excellent or very good	80%	80%	1.01 (0.94, 1.07)	73%	**0.91 (0.86, 0.97)**	65%	**0.81 (0.74, 0.88)**
Exercise in past 30 days	75%	73%	0.97 (0.91, 1.04)	73%	0.98 (0.92, 1.04)	65%	**0.87 (0.79, 0.94)**
BMI between 18.5 and 25 (normal range)	22%	27%	**1.23 (1.10, 1.37)**	22%	1.00 (0.89, 1.11)	28%	**1.28 (1.11, 1.44)**
Physical health not good for 14+ days in the past month	15%	16%	1.07 (0.91, 1.24)	19%	**1.28 (1.11, 1.46)**	24%	**1.65 (1.42, 1.89)**
Mental health not good for 14+ days in the past month	10%	15%	**1.48 (1.25, 1.70)**	18%	**1.85 (1.63, 2.08)**	20%	**1.99 (1.68, 2.29)**
Functional impairments (health interfered with daily activities for 14+ days in the past month)	21%	21%	1.02 (0.85, 1.19)	23%	1.08 (0.92, 1.24)	37%	**1.77 (1.50, 2.05)**

SOURCE: Uses data from 2015–2021 BRFSS.

NOTE: Prevalence estimates among male sexual minority groups are age-standardized to the male heterosexual group for comparison. Odds ratios are from separate logistic regression models comparing sexual identity group prevalence estimates (reference group: heterosexual veterans). Bolded text indicates significant difference from heterosexual group at $p < 0.05$.

TABLE A.5

Substance Use Outcomes Among Female Veterans, by Sexual Identity: Age-Adjusted Prevalence Estimates and Odds Ratios

Substance Use Outcome	Heterosexual Female	Lesbian or Gay Female		Bisexual Female		Other Sexual Identity Female	
	Reference Prevalence	Age-Adjusted Prevalence	OR (95% CI)	Age-Adjusted Prevalence	OR (95% CI)	Age-Adjusted Prevalence	OR (95% CI)
Current smoking	16%	29%	**1.77** **(1.51, 2.03)**	19%	1.20 (0.99, 1.42)	19%	1.19 (0.84, 1.54)
Drink any alcoholic beverages in the past 30 days	52%	62%	**1.19** **(1.07, 1.31)**	61%	**1.17** **(1.06, 1.28)**	45%	0.87 (0.70, 1.03)
Binge drinking in the past 30 days	11%	18%	**1.67** **(1.37, 1.97)**	21%	**1.97** **(1.67, 2.27)**	20%	**1.90** **(1.38, 2.42)**
Heavy alcohol consumption in the past 30 days	6%	14%	**2.39** **(1.88, 2.9)**	24%	**4.04** **(3.37, 4.7)**	6%	0.98 (0.46, 1.5)

SOURCE: Uses data from 2015–2021 BRFSS.

NOTE: Prevalence estimates among female sexual minority groups are age-standardized to the female heterosexual group for comparison. Odds ratios are from separate logistic regression models comparing sexual identity group prevalence estimates (reference group: heterosexual veterans). Bolded text indicates significant difference from heterosexual group at $p < 0.05$.

TABLE A.6

Substance Use Outcomes Among Male Veterans, by Sexual Identity: Age-Adjusted Prevalence Estimates and Odds Ratios

Substance Use Outcome	Heterosexual Male	Gay Male		Bisexual Male		Other Sexual Identity Male	
	Reference Prevalence	Age-Adjusted Prevalence	OR (95% CI)	Age-Adjusted Prevalence	OR (95% CI)	Age-Adjusted Prevalence	OR (95% CI)
Current smoking	15%	22%	**1.44** **(1.27, 1.61)**	17%	1.12 (0.98, 1.25)	18%	1.16 (0.97, 1.34)
Drink any alcoholic beverages in the past 30 days	55%	56%	1.03 (0.95, 1.10)	54%	0.98 (0.91, 1.05)	47%	**0.85** **(0.77, 0.94)**
Binge drinking in the past 30 days	14%	16%	**1.16** **(1.00, 1.31)**	15%	1.09 (0.96, 1.22)	16%	1.12 (0.93, 1.30)
Heavy alcohol consumption in the past 30 days	6%	6%	0.98 (0.75, 1.21)	7%	1.23 (1.00, 1.47)	8%	**1.40** **(1.06, 1.73)**

SOURCE: Uses data from 2015–2021 BRFSS.

NOTE: Prevalence estimates among male sexual minority groups are age-standardized to the male heterosexual group for comparison. Odds ratios are from separate logistic regression models comparing sexual identity group prevalence estimates (reference group: heterosexual veterans). Bolded text indicates significant difference from heterosexual group at $p < 0.05$.

TABLE A.7

History of Chronic Health Conditions Among Female Veterans, by Sexual Identity: Age-Adjusted Prevalence Estimates and Odds Ratios

Chronic Health Condition Outcome	Heterosexual Female Reference Prevalence	Lesbian or Gay Female Age-Adjusted Prevalence	Lesbian or Gay Female OR (95% CI)	Bisexual Female Age-Adjusted Prevalence	Bisexual Female OR (95% CI)	Other Sexual Identity Female Age-Adjusted Prevalence	Other Sexual Identity Female OR (95% CI)
Ever diagnosed with angina or CHD	4%	8%	**2.08 (1.44, 2.71)**	7%	**1.80 (1.07, 2.53)**	7%	1.72 (0.80, 2.64)
Ever diagnosed with heart attack	4%	7%	1.84 (1.23, 2.45)	8%	**2.09 (1.33, 2.86)**	10%	**2.56 (1.42, 3.7)**
Ever diagnosed with a stroke	5%	7%	1.44 (0.97, 1.91)	4%	0.89 (0.47, 1.30)	6%	1.20 (0.53, 1.87)
Ever told had depressive disorder	28%	36%	**1.25 (1.09, 1.42)**	49%	**1.73 (1.54, 1.91)**	40%	**1.41 (1.12, 1.69)**
Ever told had diabetes	10%	17%	**1.64 (1.28, 1.99)**	13%	1.31 (0.93, 1.69)	15%	1.44 (0.91, 1.96)
Ever told had kidney disease	4%	3%	0.74 (0.38, 1.10)	4%	1.08 (0.59, 1.57)	7%	1.64 (0.79, 2.5)
Ever told had arthritis, rheumatoid arthritis, gout, lupus, or fibromyalgia	35%	43%	**1.22 (1.06, 1.38)**	38%	1.09 (0.92, 1.26)	32%	0.93 (0.71, 1.15)
Ever told had COPD, emphysema, or chronic bronchitis	8%	15%	**1.85 (1.45, 2.25)**	24%	**2.94 (2.38, 3.49)**	15%	**1.84 (1.20, 2.48)**
Ever diagnosed with asthma	15%	25%	**1.61 (1.36, 1.87)**	23%	**1.52 (1.28, 1.76)**	10%	**0.66 (0.39, 0.92)**
Ever diagnosed with skin cancer	7%	11%	**1.65 (1.21, 2.09)**	8%	1.14 (0.67, 1.62)	14%	**2.07 (1.30, 2.85)**

SOURCE: Uses data from 2015–2021 BRFSS.
NOTE: Prevalence estimates among female sexual minority groups are age-standardized to the female heterosexual group for comparison. Odds ratios are from separate logistic regression models comparing sexual identity group prevalence estimates (reference group: heterosexual veterans). Bolded text indicates significant difference from heterosexual group at $p < 0.05$.

TABLE A.8

History of Chronic Health Conditions Among Male Veterans, by Sexual Identity: Age-Adjusted Prevalence Estimates and Odds Ratios

Chronic Health Condition Outcome	Heterosexual Male Reference Prevalence	Gay Male Age-Adjusted Prevalence	Gay Male OR (95% CI)	Bisexual Male Age-Adjusted Prevalence	Bisexual Male OR (95% CI)	Other Sexual Identity Male Age-Adjusted Prevalence	Other Sexual Identity Male OR (95% CI)
Ever diagnosed with angina or CHD	11%	13%	**1.26** **(1.06, 1.47)**	13%	1.19 (0.99, 1.40)	14%	**1.31** **(1.07, 1.55)**
Ever diagnosed with heart attack	11%	13%	1.14 (0.95, 1.33)	15%	**1.37** **(1.15, 1.58)**	15%	**1.36** **(1.12, 1.60)**
Ever diagnosed with a stroke	6%	9%	**1.43** **(1.14, 1.71)**	11%	**1.72** **(1.4, 2.05)**	13%	**2.15** **(1.74, 2.56)**
Ever told had depressive disorder	15%	22%	**1.47** **(1.30, 1.64)**	30%	**1.93** **(1.75, 2.12)**	28%	**1.82** **(1.59, 2.06)**
Ever told had diabetes	18%	22%	**1.19** **(1.04, 1.34)**	22%	**1.18** **(1.03, 1.34)**	20%	1.07 (0.9, 1.24)
Ever told had kidney disease	5%	6%	1.24 (0.94, 1.53)	8%	**1.58** **(1.24, 1.93)**	6%	1.17 (0.83, 1.50)
Ever told had arthritis, rheumatoid arthritis, gout, lupus, or fibromyalgia	37%	39%	1.07 (0.97, 1.17)	41%	**1.11** **(1.01, 1.21)**	38%	1.02 (0.9, 1.14)
Ever told had COPD, emphysema, or chronic bronchitis	10%	14%	**1.42** **(1.20, 1.63)**	18%	**1.77** **(1.52, 2.02)**	13%	**1.32** **(1.07, 1.57)**
Ever diagnosed with asthma	9%	12%	**1.41** **(1.19, 1.64)**	12%	**1.32** **(1.11, 1.52)**	13%	**1.50** **(1.22, 1.79)**
Ever diagnosed with skin cancer	15%	17%	1.14 (0.98, 1.31)	16%	1.07 (0.90, 1.24)	14%	0.97 (0.80, 1.15)

SOURCE: Uses data from 2015–2021 BRFSS.

NOTE: Prevalence estimates among male sexual minority groups are age-standardized to the male heterosexual group for comparison. Odds ratios are from separate logistic regression models comparing sexual identity group prevalence estimates (reference group: heterosexual veterans). Bolded text indicates significant difference from heterosexual group at $p < 0.05$.

TABLE A.9

Health Care Access Among Transgender and Cisgender Veterans: Age-Adjusted Prevalence Estimates and Odds Ratios

Health Care Access Outcome	Cisgender	Transgender	
	Reference Prevalence	Age-Adjusted Prevalence	OR (95% CI)
Has health insurance	94%	90%	0.95 (0.88, 1.02)
Has a personal health care provider	85%	89%	1.05 (0.97, 1.12)
Had checkup in past year	82%	81%	0.99 (0.92, 1.07)
Could not afford medical care in the past 12 months	7%	13%	**1.94 (1.60, 2.27)**

SOURCE: Uses data from 2015–2021 BRFSS.

NOTE: Prevalence estimates among transgender group are age-standardized to the cisgender group for comparison. Odds ratios are from separate logistic regression models comparing transgender and cisgender group prevalence estimates (reference group: cisgender veterans). Bolded text indicates significant difference from cisgender group at $p < 0.05$.

TABLE A.10

General Health Status and Health Behavior Among Transgender and Cisgender Veterans: Age-Adjusted Prevalence Estimates and Odds Ratios

Health Status and Health Behavior Outcome	Cisgender	Transgender	
	Reference Prevalence	Age-Adjusted Prevalence	OR (95% CI)
Self-reported health is excellent or very good	80%	70%	**0.88 (0.81, 0.94)**
Exercise in past 30 days	75%	60%	**0.80 (0.73, 0.87)**
BMI between 18.5 and 25 (normal range)	23%	33%	**1.42 (1.25, 1.60)**
Physical health not good for 14+ days in the past month	15%	21%	**1.43 (1.20, 1.65)**
Mental health not good for 14+ days in the past month	11%	20%	**1.83 (1.56, 2.11)**
Functional impairments (health interfered with daily activities for 14+ days in the past month)	21%	35%	**1.68 (1.42, 1.95)**

SOURCE: Uses data from 2015–2021 BRFSS.

NOTE: Prevalence estimates among transgender group are age-standardized to the cisgender group for comparison. Odds ratios are from separate logistic regression models comparing transgender and cisgender group prevalence estimates (reference group: cisgender veterans). Bolded text indicates significant difference from cisgender group at $p < 0.05$.

TABLE A.11

Substance Use Outcomes Among Transgender and Cisgender Veterans: Age-Adjusted Prevalence Estimates and Odds Ratios

Substance Use Outcome	Cisgender	Transgender	
	Reference Prevalence	Age-Adjusted Prevalence	OR (95% CI)
Current smoking	16%	23%	**1.45 (1.26, 1.65)**
Drink any alcoholic beverages in the past 30 days	54%	43%	**0.79 (0.71, 0.87)**
Drink any alcoholic beverages in the past 30 days	14%	16%	1.13 (0.96, 1.31)
Heavy alcohol consumption in the past 30 days	6%	7%	1.25 (0.95, 1.54)

SOURCE: Uses data from 2015–2021 BRFSS.

NOTE: Prevalence estimates among transgender group are age-standardized to the cisgender group for comparison. Odds ratios are from separate logistic regression models comparing transgender and cisgender group prevalence estimates (reference group: cisgender veterans). Bolded text indicates significant difference from cisgender group at $p < 0.05$.

TABLE A.12

Chronic Health Conditions Among Transgender and Cisgender Veterans: Age-Adjusted Prevalence Estimates and Odds Ratios

	Cisgender	Transgender	
Chronic Health Condition	Reference Prevalence	Age-Adjusted Prevalence	OR (95% CI)
Ever diagnosed with angina or CHD	10%	23%	**2.34 (1.98, 2.70)**
Ever diagnosed with heart attack	10%	25%	**2.46 (2.10, 2.82)**
Ever diagnosed with a stroke	6%	18%	**3.05 (2.54, 3.57)**
Ever told had depressive disorder	17%	34%	**2.00 (1.78, 2.23)**
Ever told had diabetes	18%	31%	**1.75 (1.52, 1.97)**
Ever told had kidney disease	5%	15%	**3.07 (2.49, 3.65)**
Ever told had arthritis, rheumatoid arthritis, gout, lupus, or fibromyalgia	36%	44%	**1.20 (1.08, 1.33)**
Ever told had COPD, emphysema, or chronic bronchitis	10%	22%	**2.19 (1.86, 2.52)**
Ever diagnosed with asthma	10%	20%	**2.09 (1.78, 2.4)**
Ever diagnosed with skin cancer	14%	28%	**2.03 (1.74, 2.32)**

SOURCE: Uses data from 2015–2021 BRFSS.

NOTE: Prevalence estimates among transgender group are age-standardized to the cisgender group for comparison. Odds ratios are from separate logistic regression models comparing transgender and cisgender group prevalence estimates (reference group: cisgender veterans). Bolded text indicates significant difference from cisgender group at $p < 0.05$.

Demographic Characteristics of BRFSS Veteran Respondents, by Sexual Identity and Gender Identity

Tables B.1 and B.2 show veterans' demographic characteristics by sexual and gender identity group.

TABLE B.1

Demographic Characteristics of BRFSS Veteran Respondents, by Sexual Identity

Demographic Characteristic	Heterosexual Veterans N = 179,568		Bisexual Veterans N = 2,460		Lesbian or Gay Veterans N = 2,350		Other Identity Veterans N = 1,566	
	N	(Survey %)	N	(Survey %)	N	(Survey %)	N	(Survey %)
Age								
18–24	2,446	(3)	150	(14.3)	70	(7.1)	32	(5.3)
25–34	7,936	(8.4)	356	(22.3)	176	(16.5)	122	(14.3)
35–44	11,743	(10.2)	265	(13.5)	191	(12.0)	118	(13.9)
45–54	20,572	(14.3)	324	(12.9)	347	(16.2)	153	(10.0)
55–64	30,695	(17.6)	393	(12.9)	484	(15.6)	235	(15.7)
65+	106,176	(46.4)	972	(24.1)	1,082	(32.6)	906	(40.9)
Race and ethnicity								
NH White	144,487	(74.9)	1,818	(64.8)	1,830	(68.5)	1,046	(60.1)
NH Black	12,552	(12.3)	186	(12.4)	172	(12.9)	105	(11.2)
NH other race	7,602	(3.8)	132	(5.6)	103	(3.5)	133	(5.1)
NH multiracial	4,725	(1.6)	104	(2.9)	74	(2.3)	71	(3.1)
Hispanic	6,498	(7.4)	169	(14.3)	128	(12.8)	118	(20.3)
Education								
Less than high school	5,966	(5.1)	93	(6.3)	72	(7.9)	131	(17.5)
Graduated high school	47,406	(28.6)	599	(26.5)	466	(23.8)	478	(30.5)
Some college or technical school	56,551	(38.8)	831	(42.0)	734	(38.8)	439	(31.7)
Graduated college or technical school	69,279	(27.5)	932	(25.1)	1,073	(29.5)	513	(20.3)

Table B.1—Continued

Demographic Characteristic	Heterosexual Veterans N = 179,568		Bisexual Veterans N = 2,460		Lesbian or Gay Veterans N = 2,350		Other Identity Veterans N = 1,566	
	N	(Survey %)	N	(Survey %)	N	(Survey %)	N	(Survey %)
Marital status								
Married	108,783	(63.0)	980	(36.4)	784	(36.2)	635	(38.6)
Divorced	27,509	(14.2)	473	(14.5)	293	(11.0)	233	(16.9)
Widowed	22,428	(8.8)	257	(7.3)	152	(5.6)	277	(15.7)
Separated	2,976	(2.0)	79	(3.2)	36	(1.5)	46	(2.7)
Never married	14,144	(9.9)	556	(33.3)	867	(37.9)	280	(19.6)
Unmarried couple	2,958	(2.1)	103	(5.3)	201	(7.8)	67	(6.5)
Employment status								
Employed	53,547	(37.6)	901	(41.7)	824	(40.8)	330	(27.4)
Self-employed	12,672	(7.2)	151	(7.1)	147	(8.5)	98	(8.0)
Out of work for 1+ yr	2,752	(1.7)	77	(3.2)	34	(2.1)	37	(2.6)
Out of work for <1 yr	2,581	(1.8)	75	(4.6)	60	(3.8)	33	(3.8)
Homemaker	1,105	(0.9)	43	(2.6)	16	(0.6)	22	(1.9)
Student	1,514	(1.7)	83	(8.1)	47	(3.6)	26	(2.1)
Retired	94,591	(43.1)	911	(25.9)	1,039	(33.8)	816	(40.7)
Unable to work	9,886	(6.0)	205	(6.7)	170	(6.7)	190	(13.5)

Table B.1—Continued

Demographic Characteristic	Heterosexual Veterans N = 179,568		Bisexual Veterans N = 2,460		Lesbian or Gay Veterans N = 2,350		Other Identity Veterans N = 1,566	
	N	(Survey %)	N	(Survey %)	N	(Survey %)	N	(Survey %)
Income								
Less than $15K	7,710	(4.0)	201	(9.1)	149	(9.7)	169	(10.4)
$15K to <$25K	19,345	(10.3)	376	(16.7)	336	(14.2)	281	(17.8)
$25K to <$35K	17,347	(9.1)	296	(11.5)	242	(10.7)	184	(13.0)
$35K to < $50K	25,661	(13.7)	381	(18.1)	356	(13.5)	187	(10.7)
$50K to < $100K	80,154	(47.1)	875	(31.5)	974	(38.7)	461	(32.3)
$100K to < $200K	4,514	(2.4)	55	(1.8)	72	(3.4)	26	(1.4)
$200K+	1,043	(0.5)	13	(0.5)	13	(0.5)	10	(1.3)
Missing	23,794	(12.9)	263	(10.9)	208	(9.3)	248	(13.2)
Sex								
Male	163,163	(90.5)	1,825	(68.1)	1,645	(66.6)	1,317	(77.8)
Female	16,354	(9.5)	632	(31.9)	702	(33.4)	248	(22.2)

SOURCE: Uses data from 2015–the 2021 BRFSS.

NOTE: NH = non Hispanic. Ns are not survey weighted.

TABLE B.2

Demographic Characteristics of BRFSS Veteran Respondents, by Gender Identity

Demographic Characteristic	Cisgender Veterans N = 184,957		Transgender Veterans N = 987	
	N	(Survey %)	N	(Survey %)
Age				
18–24	2,711	(3.2)	32	(9.8)
25–34	8,667	(8.7)	56	(11.8)
35–44	12,432	(10.3)	75	(11.2)
45–54	21,645	(14.3)	116	(11.5)
55–64	32,103	(17.4)	203	(23.5)
65+	111,142	(46.1)	505	(32.2)
Race and ethnicity				
NH White	151,213	(74.6)	676	(56.3)
NH Black	13,143	(12.3)	91	(14.5)
NH other race	8,110	(3.9)	71	(4.7)
NH multiracial	5,001	(1.7)	47	(1.9)
Hispanic	6,961	(7.6)	75	(22.5)
Education				
Less than high school	6,413	(5.2)	94	(22.0)
Graduated high school	49,820	(28.6)	308	(29.1)
Some college or technical school	59,303	(38.7)	306	(33.6)
Graduated college or technical school	72,736	(27.4)	273	(15.3)
Marital status				
Married	112,740	(62.2)	474	(43.9)
Divorced	28,784	(14.1)	168	(15.2)
Widowed	23,612	(8.8)	149	(14.7)
Separated	3,147	(2.0)	21	(1.9)
Never married	16,091	(10.7)	141	(21.2)
Unmarried couple	3,363	(2.3)	27	(3.1)

Table B.2—Continued

Demographic Characteristic	Cisgender Veterans N = 184,957		Transgender Veterans N = 987	
	N	(Survey %)	N	(Survey %)
Employment status				
Employed	56,172	(37.5)	268	(31.2)
Self-employed	13,276	(7.3)	70	(5.9)
Out of work for 1+ year	2,911	(1.8)	32	(4.7)
Out of work for < 1 year	2,772	(1.9)	18	(2.1)
Homemaker	1,198	(0.9)	16	(1.3)
Student	1,681	(1.8)	10	(1.4)
Retired	99,105	(42.9)	455	(36.9)
Unable to work	10,530	(6.0)	112	(16.4)
Income				
< $15K	8,330	(4.2)	91	(16.7)
$15K to <$25K	20,686	(10.4)	156	(17.5)
$25K to <$35K	18,337	(9.2)	127	(11.3)
$35K to <$50K	26,852	(13.7)	136	(9.5)
$50K to <$100K	83,053	(46.5)	317	(28.4)
$100K to <$200K	4,752	(2.4)	19	(1.5)
$200K+	1,090	(0.5)	7	(0.8)
Missing	25,600	(13.2)	134	(14.3)
Sex				
Male	170,483	(89.7)	764	(73.4)
Female	18,153	(10.3)	215	(26.6)

SOURCE: Uses data from 2015–2021 BRFSS.

NOTE: NH = non Hispanic. Ns are not survey weighted.

BRFSS Response Rates, by State

Table C.1 shows state BRFSS response rates for 2015–2021.

TABLE C.1

State-Specific Combined Landline and Cell Phone BRFSS Response Rates, 2015–2021

State	2015	2016	2017	2018	2019	2020	2021
AL	38.8	37.8	36.2	47.2	45.9	42.4	44.6
AK	54.2	57.0	54.0	62.7	61.4	63.8	59.4
AZ	43.7	43.3	43.0	53.5	54.7	46.8	43.3
AR	48.9	48.0	48.0	55.6	59.2	50.0	46.4
CA	33.9	31.1	31.4	38.8	40.2	38.7	41.8
CO	55.2	56.0	51.8	54.2	52.9	50.9	43.4
CT	38.6	34.9	37.1	44.2	44.5	40.9	36.2
DE	43.6	43.0	38.4	39.8	38.2	38.5	39.1
DC	37.9	35.9	36.8	48.0	40.6	45.1	42.3
FL	37.0	52.4	46.5	49.3	44.3	40.1	*
GA	47.6	48.6	44.8	43.6	42.2	39.1	36.1
HI	42.2	43.0	43.0	43.6	42.8	42.0	39.7
ID	50.0	51.4	47.9	53.9	42.0	51.0	51.5
IL	37.9	33.9	30.6	41.1	38.6	49.5	47.1
IN	42.6	41.5	39.3	49.1	46.2	43.4	38.4
IA	55.5	53.4	51.8	55.4	58.7	55.5	52.6
KS	56.2	54.5	52.6	58.8	57.7	57.8	51.5
KY	59.0	58.2	56.1	59.3	60.3	43.3	46.8
LA	41.2	30.7	34.0	39.1	42.3	37.0	37.7
ME	52.9	52.2	49.3	55.0	60.1	54.5	51.9
MD	39.7	41.7	38.2	44.7	45.0	45.8	38.9
MA	39.8	37.0	32.8	46.8	50.6	48.8	47.4
MI	49.9	49.6	47.3	50.9	51.5	48.3	48.0
MN	56.7	54.7	51.5	51.0	47.6	45.5	43.4
MS	43.9	41.2	46.4	56.2	57.4	67.2	55.9
MO	52.9	51.4	48.2	55.7	56.2	57.8	52.4
MT	56.8	56.5	54.2	58.1	56.4	50.4	47.5
NE	56.3	54.9	53.4	56.8	57.3	56.1	51.5
NV	46.0	41.3	44.6	48.5	51.8	47.9	41.4

Table C.1—Continued

State	2015	2016	2017	2018	2019	2020	2021
NH	42.7	42.2	42.0	50.0	49.4	49.2	45.0
NJ	46.6	44.8	38.6	42.9	*	34.5	35.4
NM	52.5	51.8	48.4	50.5	52.2	52.3	51.4
NY	34.5	36.3	32.9	40.1	37.3	36.1	36.2
NC	42.9	39.3	35.9	43.5	40.8	44.8	43.4
ND	58.9	58.6	56.9	58.6	60.8	55.6	53.5
OH	57.6	55.2	51.7	51.7	46.4	42.9	43.5
OK	47.2	47.0	48.2	51.6	55.0	52.4	47.2
OR	50.0	56.6	45.9	39.8	46.5	50.1	43.3
PA	44.5	42.5	41.6	44.4	46.6	40.0	41.2
RI	38.1	37.1	37.9	41.3	43.6	39.1	35.1
SC	51.5	47.3	45.8	49.9	54.6	47.9	39.3
SD	60.4	59.3	57.2	67.2	73.1	61.2	60.5
TN	38.6	36.7	35.1	39.0	42.0	39.1	36.8
TX	34.4	36.7	40.0	48.9	46.3	40.6	35.6
UT	61.1	58.4	56.4	57.0	54.8	55.4	47.3
VT	50.2	45.1	39.9	48.9	49.3	46.8	42.7
VA	53.7	50.9	46.6	46.6	43.4	41.5	38.9
WA	36.0	39.3	39.6	50.0	47.1	47.6	44.0
WV	48.9	45.8	42.8	46.7	49.6	47.6	46.0
WI	45.0	49.8	46.1	51.6	53.3	53.8	52.1
WY	42.6	65.0	64.1	64.1	60.8	55.9	49.5
GU	48.9	46.1	45.4	41.5	48.8	51.0	23.5
PR	52.5	55.6	53.4	52.7	51.5	47.9	49.7
VI	NA	56.1	NA	NA	NA	NA	50.1
Minimum	33.9	30.7	30.6	38.8	37.3	34.5	23.5
Maximum	61.1	65.0	64.1	67.2	73.1	67.2	60.5
Median	47.2	47.1	45.9	49.9	49.4	47.9	44.0

NOTE: NA indicates that the U.S. Virgin Islands did not participate in BRFSS that year. * indicates that a state did not collect the minimum amount of data that year to be included in the BRFSS public-use data set.

Details of Sex, Sex at Birth, and SOGI Items in BRFSS

This appendix presents tables (D.1, D.2, and D.3) and a narrative description of additional methodological details for questions in the BRFSS that were used to assess respondents' sex, sex at birth, and sexual orientation and gender identity during survey years 2015–2021.

Sex: In our analyses, *sex* (male or female) is based on the calculated sex variable in the BRFSS public use data. Assessment of sex in BRFSS changed across our study years. Sex was based on interviewer-recorded sex in 2015 and self-reported sex in 2016–2021. In 2018, respondents were asked "What is your sex?" and could answer *male, female, don't know/ not sure*, or *refuse to answer*. In 2019–2021, the question was rephrased to "Are you male or female?" and included response options of *don't know/not sure* and *refuse to answer*. As reported in the BRFSS documentation, respondent sex is never imputed; however, with the addition of sex at birth, "if the responses to sex at birth and sex are reported differently, sex at birth responses will supersede sex in the calculated variable." (CDC, undated).

Sexual identity: In 2014–2017, sexual identity was assessed on the optional SOGI module with the item: "Do you consider yourself to be" with the response options *straight, lesbian or gay, bisexual, other*, or *don't know/not sure*. In 2018–2021, sexual identity was assessed with the item: "Which of the following best represents how you think of yourself?" with response options *gay* (for male respondents) / *lesbian or gay* (female respondents), *straight, that is, not gay, bisexual, something else*, or *I don't know the answer*. In these analyses, individuals were classified into four sexual identity groups using these items: gay/lesbian, bisexual, other identity, and heterosexual.

Gender identity: Transgender veterans were identified based on either (1) the transgender identity question in the optional SOGI module (2015–2021) or (2) based on the optional Sex at Birth module (2019–2021). In the SOGI module, respondents are asked "Do you consider yourself to be transgender?" In our analyses, all individuals who responded *yes* were classified as transgender. We note that in the SOGI module, if respondents answer affirmatively, they are then able to identify as *transgender, male-to-female; transgender, female-to-male;* or *transgender, gender nonconforming*. We note that we were not able to examine differences among transgender respondents based on specific gender identities because of the limited sample size. In 2019, the optional Sex at Birth module was introduced. This module asks "What was your sex at birth? Was it male or female?" In our analyses, we also classified individuals as transgender if their reported sex at birth did not match the BRFSS sex variable (e.g., sex at birth recorded as male, sex at birth reported as female). All individuals who were not identified as transgender were classified as cisgender.

TABLE D.1

Sex, Sex at Birth, and SOGI Questions of the BRFSS for Survey Years 2015 Through 2021

Sex (Demographics Section) 2015	What is your sex? 1 = Male 2 = Female [Interviewer instruction: "Ask only if necessary"]
Sex (Demographics Section) 2016–2018	Are you male or female? [Interviewers required to ask participants]
Sex (Screening Section) 2019–2021	Are you male or female?
SOGI Optional Module 2015–2017	Do you consider yourself to be: 1 = Straight 2 = Lesbian or gay 3 = Bisexual 4 = Other 7 = Don't know/Not sure 9 = Refused Do you consider yourself to be transgender? If yes, ask "Do you consider yourself to be 1 = male-to-female 2 = female-to-male 3 = gender non-conforming?
SOGI Optional Module 2018–2021	Which of the following best represents how you think of yourself? *[For male respondents]* 1 = Gay 2 = Straight, that is, not gay 3 = Bisexual 4 = Something else 7 = I don't know the answer 9 = Refused Which of the following best represents how you think of yourself? *[For female respondents]* 1 = Lesbian or Gay 2 = Straight, that is, not gay 3 = Bisexual 4 = Something else 7 = I don't know the answer 9 = Refused Do you consider yourself to be transgender? 1 = Yes, Transgender, male-to-female 2 = Yes, Transgender, female-to-male 3 = Yes, Transgender, gender nonconforming 4 = No
Sex at Birth Optional Module (may be included with demographics section) 2019–2021	What was your sex at birth? Was it male or female?

TABLE D.2

State Inclusion of the Optional BRFSS SOGI Module, 2015–2021

State	2015	2016	2017	2018	2019	2020	2021
AL							
AK					X	X	X
AZ				X	X		
AR						X	X
CA		X	X			X	
CO	X				X	X	X
CT	X	X	X	X	X	X	X
DE	X	X	X	X	X		
DC							
FL			X	X	X		*
GA	X	X	X		X	X	X
HI	X	X	X	X	X	X	X
ID	X	X		X	X	X	X
IL	X	X	X	X		X	X
IN	X	X	X	X	X	X	X
IA	X	X	X		X	X	X
KS	X				X	X	X
KY		X					X
LA		X	X	X	X	X	X
ME							
MD	X			X	X		
MA	X	X	X			X	X
MI						X	X
MN	X	X	X	X	X	X	X
MS		X	X	X	X		X
MO	X	X		X	X		X
MT			X	X	X	X	X
NE							
NV	X	X	X	X			X
NH							

Table D.2—Continued

State	2015	2016	2017	2018	2019	2020	2021
NJ					X*	X	X
NM						X	X
NY	X	X	X	X	X	X	
NC			X	X	X	X	X
ND							
OH	X	X	X	X	X	X	X
OK			X	X	X	X	X
OR							
PA	X	X	X	X			X
RI		X	X	X	X	X	X
SC			X	X	X	X	
SD							
TN				X	X		
TX	X	X	X	X	X	X	X
UT				X	X	X	X
VT		X	X	X	X	X	X
VA	X	X	X	X	X	X	X
WA		X	X	X	X	X	X
WV	X			X	X	X	X
WI	X	X	X	X	X		
WY							
GU	X	X	X	X	X	X	
PR							
VI	NA		NA	NA	NA	NA	
Total	23	26	28	32	34	32	33

NOTE: BRFSS is conducted in all 50 U.S. states, the District of Columbia, Guam, Puerto Rico, and the U.S. Virgin Islands. A green-shaded X indicates that the state in question included the BRFSS SOGI module (the table does not include state-specific SOGI questions). NA indicates that the U.S. Virgin Islands did not participate in BRFSS that year. * indicates that a state did not collect the minimum amount of data that year to be included in the BRFSS public-use data set.

TABLE D.3

State Inclusion of the Optional BRFSS Sex at Birth Module, 2019–2021

State	2019	2020	2021
AL			
AK			
AZ			
AR			
CA		X	
CO			
CT			
DE			
DC			
FL			
GA		X	X
HI	X	X	X
ID			
IL			
IN			
IA		X	X
KS			X
KY			
LA	X	X	X
ME			
MD			
MA			
MI			
MN	X	X	X
MS			
MO			
MT			
NE			
NV			

Table D.3—Continued

State	2019	2020	2021
NH			
NJ			
NM		X	X
NY	X	X	
NC			
ND			
OH			X
OK			
OR			
PA	X		
RI			
SC			
SD			
TN			
TX			
UT	X	X	X
VT		X	
VA			
WA			
WV			
WI			
WY			
GU			
PR			
VI	NA	NA	
Total	6	10	9

NOTE: BRFSS is conducted in all 50 U.S. states, the District of Columbia, Guam, Puerto Rico, and the U.S. Virgin Islands. A green-shaded X indicates that the state in question included the BRFSS Sex at Birth module. NA indicates that the U.S. Virgin Islands did not participate in BRFSS that year.

Abbreviations

BMI	body mass index
BRFSS	Behavioral Risk Factor Surveillance System
CDC	Centers for Disease Control and Prevention
CHD	coronary heart disease
CI	confidence interval
COPD	chronic obstructive pulmonary disease
DADT	Don't Ask, Don't Tell
DoD	U.S. Department of Defense
LGBTQ+	lesbian, gay, bisexual, transgender, queer, and other sexual and gender minority
MAP	Movement Advancement Project
OR	odds ratio
SOGI	Sexual Orientation and Gender Identity
VA	Department of Veterans Affairs
VHA	Veterans Health Administration

References

American Civil Liberties Union, "Mapping Attacks on LGBTQ Rights in U.S. State Legislatures in 2024," webpage, last updated March 15, 2024. As of March 15, 2024: https://www.aclu.org/legislative-attacks-on-lgbtq-rights-2024

Blosnich, John R., George R. Brown, Jillian C. Shipherd, Michael Kauth, Rebecca I. Piegari, and Robert M. Bossarte, "Prevalence of Gender Identity Disorder and Suicide Risk Among Transgender Veterans Utilizing Veterans Health Administration Care," *American Journal of Public Health*, Vol. 103, No. 10, October 2013.

Blosnich, John R., Mary C. Marsiglio, Shasha Gao, Adam J. Gordon, Jillian C. Shipherd, Michael Kauth, George R. Brown, and Michael J. Fine, "Mental Health of Transgender Veterans in US States With and Without Discrimination and Hate Crime Legal Protection," *American Journal of Public Health*, Vol. 106, No. 3, March 2016.

Brown, George R., and Kenneth T. Jones, "Racial Health Disparities in a Cohort of 5,135 Transgender Veterans," *Journal of Racial and Ethnic Health Disparities*, Vol. 1, No. 4, December 2014.

Burgess, Claire, C. B. Klemt Craig, and Cary L. Klemmer, "Sexual and Gender Minority Marginalization in Military Contexts," in Emily M. Lund, Claire Burgess, and Andy J. Johnson, eds., *Violence Against LGBTQ+ Persons: Research, Practice, and Advocacy*, Springer, 2021.

Carey, Felicia R., Cynthia A. LeardMann, Keren Lehavot, Isabel G. Jacobson, Claire A. Kolaja, Valerie A. Stander, and Rudolph P. Rull, "Health Disparities Among Lesbian, Gay, and Bisexual Service Members and Veterans," *American Journal of Preventive Medicine*, Vol. 63, No. 4, October 2022.

CDC—*See* Centers for Disease Control and Prevention.

Centers for Disease Control and Prevention, "Statistical Brief: Using Sexual Orientation, Gender Identity, Sex, and Sex-at-Birth Variables in Analysis," survey guide, undated.

Centers for Disease Control and Prevention, "Behavioral Risk Factor Surveillance System: BRFSS Questionnaires," webpage, last reviewed August 29, 2023. As of March 15, 2024: https://www.cdc.gov/brfss/questionnaires/index.htm

Cicero, Ethan C., Sari L. Reisner, Elizabeth I. Merwin, Janice C. Humphreys, and Susan G. Silva, "Application of Behavioral Risk Factor Surveillance System Sampling Weights to Transgender Health Measurement," *Nursing Research*, Vol. 69, No. 4, July–August 2020.

Committee on Lesbian, Gay, Bisexual and Transgender Health Issues and Research Gaps and Opportunities, Institute of Medicine, *The Health of Lesbian, Gay, Bisexual, and Transgender People: Building a Foundation for Better Understanding*, 2011.

Davis, Nickolas B., "'Don't Say Gay': The Influence of State Political Factors," *Sexuality, Gender and Policy*, Vol. 6, No. 2, May 2023.

Dawson, Lindsey, Jennifer Kates, and Anthony Damico, "The Affordable Care Act and Insurance Coverage Changes by Sexual Orientation," Kaiser Family Foundation, January 18, 2018.

DoD—*See* U.S. Department of Defense.

Downing, Janelle, Kerith Conron, Jody L. Herman, and John R. Blosnich, "Transgender and Cisgender US Veterans Have Few Health Differences," *Health Affairs*, Vol. 37, No. 7, July 2018.

Draper, Debra A., *VA Health Care: Better Data Needed to Assess the Health Outcomes of Lesbian, Gay, Bisexual, and Transgender Veterans*, report to Congressional Committees, U.S. Government Accountability Office, GAO-21-69, October 2020.

Dwyer, Devin, and Sarah Herndon, " Pentagon, States Begin New Push to Help LGBTQ Veterans Kicked Out of Military," ABC News, December 24, 2023.

Garcia, Robert, Mark Pocan, and Chris Pappas, letter to the Secretary of Defense Lloyd J. Austin III, Congress of the United States, January 25, 2024.

Goldenberg, Tamar, Sari L. Reisner, Gary W. Harper, Kristi E. Gamarel, and Rob Stephenson, "State Policies and Healthcare Use Among Transgender People in the U.S.," *American Journal of Preventive Medicine*, Vol. 59, No. 2, August 2020.

Grogan, Nathalie, Emma Moore, Brent Peabody, Margaret Seymour, and Kayla M. Williams, *New York State Minority Veteran Needs Assessment*, Center for New American Security, February 20, 2020.

Hatzenbuehler, Mark L., Katherine M. Keyes, and Deborah S. Hasin, "State-Level Policies and Psychiatric Morbidity in Lesbian, Gay, and Bisexual Populations," *American Journal of Public Health*, Vol. 99, No. 12, 2009.

Human Rights Campaign, *2022 State Equality Index: A Review of State Legislation Affecting the Lesbian, Gay, Bisexual, Transgender and Queer Community and a Look Ahead in 2023*, 2023.

James, Sandy E., Jody L. Herman, Susan Rankin, Mara Keisling, Lisa Mottet, and Ma'ayan Anafi, *The Report of the 2015 U.S. Transgender Survey*, National Center for Transgender Equality, December 2016.

Kauth, Michael R., Terri L. Barrera, and David M. Latini, "Lesbian, Gay, and Transgender Veterans' Experiences in the Veterans Health Administration: Positive Signs and Room for Improvement, *Psychological Services*, Vol. 16, No. 2, May 2019.

Kheel, Rebecca, "Veterans Discharged Under 'Don't Ask, Don't Tell' and Earlier Bans Sue Pentagon to Correct Records," Military.com, August 9, 2023.

Kondo, Karli, Allison Low, Teresa Everson, Christine D. Gordon, Stephanie Veazie, Crystal C. Lozier, Michele Freeman, Makalapua Motu'apuaka, Aaron Mendelson, Mark Friesen, Robin Paynter, Caroline Friesen, Johanna Anderson, Erin Boundy, Somnath Saha, Ana Quiñones, and Devan Kansagara, "Health Disparities in Veterans: A Map of the Evidence," *Medical Care*, Vol. 55, Supp. 9, September 2017.

Lenson, Jillian, "Litigation Primer Attacking State 'No Promo Homo' Laws: Why 'Don't Say Gay' Is Not O.K.," *Tulane Journal of Law and Sexuality*, Vol. 24, 2015.

MAP—*See* Movement Advancement Project.

Mark, Katharine M., Kathleen McNamara, Rachael Gribble, Rebecca Rhead, Marie-Louise Sharp, Sharon A. M. Stevelink, Alix Schwartz, Carl Castro, and Nicola T. Fear, "The Health and Well-Being of LGBTQ Serving and Ex-Serving Personnel: A Narrative Review," *International Review of Psychiatry*, Vol. 31, No. 1, February 2019.

Meffert, Brienna N., Danielle M. Morabito, Danielle A. Sawicki, Catherine Hausman, Steven M. Southwick, Robert H. Pietrzak, and Adrienne J. Heinz, "US Veterans Who Do and Do Not Utilize Veterans Affairs Health Care Services: Demographic, Military, Medical, and Psychosocial Characteristics," *Primary Care Companion for CNS Disorders*, Vol. 21, No. 1, January 2019.

Meyer, Ilan H., "Prejudice, Social Stress, and Mental Health in Lesbian, Gay, and Bisexual Populations: Conceptual Issues and Research Evidence," *Psychological Bulletin*, Vol. 129, No. 5, September 2003.

Movement Advancement Project, "Medicaid Coverage of Transgender-Related Health Care, " webpage, last updated March 14, 2024. As of March 17, 2024: https://www.lgbtmap.org/equality-maps/healthcare/medicaid

Movement Advancement Project, *Mapping LGBT Equality in America*, May 28, 2015.

Movement Advancement Project, *LGBTQ Policy Spotlight: Mapping LGBTQ Equality: 2010 to 2020*, 2020.

Murphy, Charlotte N., Christian Delles, Eleanor Davies, and Paul J. Connelly, "Cardiovascular Disease in Transgender Individuals," *Atherosclerosis*, Vol. 348, November 2023.

National Defense Research Institute, *Sexual Orientation and U.S. Military Personnel Policy: An Update of RAND's 1993 Study*, RAND Corporation, MG-1056-OSD, 2010. As of January 25, 2024: https://www.rand.org/pubs/monographs/MG1056.html

National Institutes of Health, "NIH Style Guide: Sex, Gender, and Sexuality," webpage, last reviewed January 17, 2024. As of March 17, 2024: https://www.nih.gov/nih-style-guide/sex-gender-sexuality

National Institutes of Health, Sexual and Gender Minority Research Office, "Sexual & Gender Minority Health Disparities Framework," last updated June 2021.

Patterson, Charlotte J., Martín-José Sepúlveda, and Jordyn White, eds., *Understanding the Well-Being of LGBTQI+ Populations*, National Academies of Sciences, Engineering, and Medicine, 2020.

Purnell, Jonathan Q., "Definitions, Classification, and Epidemiology of Obesity," in Kenneth R. Feingold, Bradley Anawalt, Marc R. Blackman, Alison Boyce, George Chrousos, Emiliano Corpas, Wouter W. de Herder, Ketan Dhatariya, Kathleen Dungan, Johannes Hofland, et al., eds., *Endotext*, last updated May 4, 2023.

Riley, Noah C., John R. Blosnich, Todd M. Bear, and Sari L. Reisner, "Vocal Timbre and the Classification of Respondent Sex in US Phone-Based Surveys," *American Journal of Public Health*, Vol. 107, No. 8, August 2017.

Robertson, Nick, "More Than 275 Bills Targeting LGBTQ Rights Flood State Legislatures," *The Hill*, January 16, 2024.

Schaefer, Agnes Gereben, Radha Iyengar Plumb, Srikanth Kadiyala, Jennifer Kavanagh, Charles C. Engel, Kayla M. Williams, and Amii M. Kress, *Assessing the Implications of Allowing Transgender Personnel to Serve Openly*, RAND Corporation, RR-1530-OSD, 2016. As of January 30, 2024: https://www.rand.org/pubs/research_reports/RR1530.html

Shane, Leo, III, "GOP Budget Bill Would Ban Abortions, Transgender Services at VA," *Military Times*, June 13, 2023.

Shane, Leo, III, "Transgender Vets Sue VA to Force Move on Gender Confirmation Surgeries," *Military Times*, January 25, 2024.

Substance Abuse and Mental Health Services Administration, *Lesbian, Gay, and Bisexual Behavioral Health: Results from the 2021 and 2022 National Surveys on Drug Use and Health*, No. PEP23-07-01-001, 2023.

Suter, Tara, "Garcia Presses Pentagon for Action on Veterans Discharged Under 'Don't Ask, Don't Tell,'" *The Hill*, January 26, 2024.

Thomas, Zora, "Congress Is Trying to Deny Health Care to Transgender Veterans," American Civil Liberties Union, October 16, 2023.

Tran, Nguyen K., Kellan E. Baker, Elle Lett, and Ayden I. Scheim, "State-Level Heterogeneity in Associations Between Structural Stigma and Individual Health Care Access: A Multilevel Analysis of Transgender Adults in the United States," *Journal of Health Services Research and Policy*, Vol. 28, No. 2, April 2023.

U.S. Department of Defense, "Don't Ask, Don't Tell Resources," webpage, undated. As of March 17, 2024:
https://www.defense.gov/Spotlights/Dont-Ask-Dont-Tell-Resources/

U.S. Department of Veterans Affairs, "Patient Care Services: VHA LGBTQ+ Health Program," webpage, undated. As of March 17, 2024:
https://www.patientcare.va.gov/lgbt/

U.S. Department of Veterans Affairs, "VA Health Systems Research: Improving Healthcare for LGBTQ+ Veterans," webpage, June 2022. As of March 31, 2024:
https://www.hsrd.research.va.gov/news/feature/lgbtq-healthcare-0622.cfm

U.S. Department of Veterans Affairs, Office of Resolution Management, Diversity and Inclusion, "LGBTQ+ Program," webpage, last updated June 29, 2022. As of March 17, 2024:
https://www.va.gov/ORMDI/DiversityInclusion/LGBT.asp

White, Bradley Patrick, Nadia N. Abuelezam, Holly B. Fontenot, and Corrine Y. Jurgens, "Exploring Relationships Between State-Level LGBTQ Inclusivity and BRFSS Indicators of Mental Health and Risk Behaviors: A Secondary Analysis," Vol. 29, No. 3, *Journal of the American Psychiatric Nurses Association*, May–June 2023.

White House, "Fact Sheet: Biden-Harris Administration is Supporting America's Veterans and Their Families, Caregivers, and Survivors," Executive Office of the President, November 11, 2022.

Wiessner, Daniel, "LGBTQ Veterans Sue US Military over Biased Discharges," Reuters, August 9, 2023.

Williams, Kayla, "Bill Would Ban Care for Transgender Veterans; the Scientific and Medical Consensus Tells Us That's a Mistake," *RAND Blog*, July 5, 2023. As of March 31, 2024:
https://www.rand.org/pubs/commentary/2023/07/
bill-would-ban-care-for-transgender-veterans-the-scientific.html